MINISTRY DELUGE

MINISTRY VELOCITY

The Power for Leadership Momentum

Wayne Schmidt

wesleyan
publishing
house

Indianapolis, Indiana

Copyright © 2010 by Wesleyan Publishing House
Published by Wesleyan Publishing House
Indianapolis, Indiana 46250
Printed in the United States of America
ISBN: 978-0-89827-468-4

Chapters 1–8 of this book were originally released as *Leading When God is Moving* and *Ministry Momentum: How to Get It, Keep It, and Use It in Your Church*. Chapters 9–16 were originally released as *Lead On: Why Churches Stall and How Leaders Get Them Going*.

CONTENTS

FOREWORD

You've been there—alone in your office, perhaps tired and frustrated, wondering, *Why doesn't God do something?* As leaders in local churches, we often invest ourselves deeply in ministry. We preach, counsel, pray, and lead with great tenacity. Then, too often, we're disappointed when God doesn't respond to our efforts in the way we'd hoped. Our ministry results are less spectacular than we'd envisioned. There are more setbacks that we'd ever dreamed. There is progress—but it's slow.

I don't know a pastor who hasn't yearned to be more fruitful in ministry. And I know few who haven't felt disappointed or discouraged when those hoped-for results seemed slow in coming.

The apostle Peter could have been speaking to you and me when he said, "The Lord is not slow in keeping his promise, as some understand slowness. He is patient . . ." (2 Pet. 3:9). One of the most freeing discoveries that I've made about ministry is that God builds his church in his time. It's pointless to run ahead of God—and often painful. We're always better off to discover God's schedule and work within it rather than trying to impose ours upon him.

Joshua, the conquering hero of the Promised Land, learned that lesson early in his career. Every success seemed to be followed by a failure, every opportunity accompanied by conflict. In time, though, we see the divine pattern emerge through Joshua's life. We discover that God accomplishes his work through setbacks as well as through successes, and that conflict and even failure provide the opportunities for leaders to grow, develop other leaders around them, and ultimately move forward to even greater fruitfulness. Through Joshua's life, we see that God is always working, even when he seems to be doing nothing at all.

My friend Wayne Schmidt is a rare Christian leader who understands the difference between patience and idleness and who knows how to use God's apparent down time to good advantage. With astounding honesty, he recounts the painful mistakes and joyous discoveries that have formed him into the godly and effective pastor that he is. And Wayne's beneath-the-surface look at Joshua's leadership reveals the surprising mix of patience and boldness that enabled this uncanny leader to do what we have all dreamed of—claiming new territory for the King.

This book is a manual for any church leader who has ever been frustrated by the seemingly slow pace of growth. Let these insights encourage and convict you as you lead God's people—sometimes fast, sometimes slow, always in his time.

—Bill Hybels

INTRODUCTION

"I have brought you glory on earth by completing the work you gave me to do" (John 17:4). Jesus passionately prayed these words as he approached the conclusion of his earthly ministry. It's become my life verse, and out of it arises three questions I regularly ask myself:

- Who gets the glory? "I have brought *you* glory on earth . . ."
- Who sets the finish line? ". . . by *completing* the work . . ."
- Who gives the assignments? ". . . the work *you gave me* to do" (emphasis added).

This verse and the questions that arise out of it are navigational beacons that still guide me after thirty years of ministry.

Recently, God surprised me with a finish line I didn't see coming. When I went to Kentwood, Michigan, in 1979, to plant Kentwood Community Church, it was an answer to prayer. That prayer was prompted by a challenge from Laurel Buckingham in my senior year at Marion College (now Indiana Wesleyan University). Buckingham said to "pray that God will call you to a community where you could spend a lifetime." This was a novel challenge in a day when pastors thought only in terms of being called to a church, not a community, and the average pastoral tenure was three to five years.

So, I fully anticipated living out my lifetime call in the community of Kentwood. At the thirty-year mark of serving that first ring suburb of Grand Rapids, Michigan, I was as energized as ever by the ministry context in which God had placed me. Our community had changed over those thirty years from about 98 percent Anglo (and mostly Dutch) to an ethnic minority population of nearly 40 percent. Its rich diversity was reflected in our local schools, where the students came from over fifty different nations and were exposed to nearly sixty languages. The high school graduation ceremony felt like a United Nations event.

I worked with our church board to prayerfully anticipate what God might do through the church in the next decade. We were early in the journey of becoming a multiethnic church and passionately engaged in the dream of a church that would reflect both heaven (Rev. 7:9) and our community. I was blessed to serve with a constellation of colleagues on our church staff, but I was equally energized by lay leaders who gave their best to permeate our diverse community with the good news of Jesus Christ and to plant churches on a nearly annual basis in the core city and surrounding suburbs.

But again, God surprised me. It first happened in a conversation with a dear friend from church. Kyle and Petra, a wonderful African-American couple, had moved to our community as newlyweds a decade earlier. They were young professionals, successful even in the early stages of their careers. They immersed themselves in ministry as volunteers, and in the process, God placed a call upon Kyle's heart to enter vocational ministry. He went to seminary, and we stayed in touch. I was delighted when God led him to return to Kentwood Community Church as our outreach pastor in 2006.

Kyle and I met at a local coffee shop on January 20, 2009. He shared with me a prompting he sensed in our Christmas Eve services a few weeks earlier that 2009 was the year he was to begin to prepare to be a senior pastor. And in that conversation, I sensed a prompting of the Spirit to ask, "Kyle, do you feel called to this community and to this church?" Over the next few months, further conversations, inspired by an intense season of prayer, brought me to the conclusion that God had set my finish line at Kentwood Community Church, and that I would soon pass the torch to my dear friend and colleague in ministry.

Once again, I was privileged to join God in something he was orchestrating, but this time, it was accompanied by intense grief. I knew I was being released from the community and church that I loved; the tears I shed every time I thought of it were evidence of it. This grief was accompanied by the uncertainty of not knowing exactly what God had next for me. I felt as if I was in a free fall, but I also sensed God was doing a deep work in my life to cull out seeds of insecurity that periodically plagued me. He was creating a dependency on him and an identity in him that could not be compromised by just moving on to what was next.

This transition tested how grounded I was in Scripture. Joshua's journey, foundational to the insights in *Ministry Velocity*, is unveiled in the narrative of the Old Testament book that bears his name. Principles rooted in the inspired pages of the Bible are timeless and transcendent. They are not bound to a particular culture but can be applied—and have authority—in all contexts, situations, and seasons. As you read this book, note the roots of Scripture. I hope there will be many occasions when you put down this book and pick up the Bible, God's Word, and allow it to speak to you. I also hope that you'll process with others the insights you gain, not only in official groups such as boards, task forces, or ministry teams, but also in coffee-shop conversations with people who journey with you. His Word, I trust reflected in these words recorded here, will be what remains.

In recent days, as I've witnessed the walks of others and sought to be faithful in the midst of change, my heart is captured by the critical importance of being and remaining a follower. It's the initial call of discipleship ("Come, follow me . . ." [Matt. 19:21]) and the enduring discipline of any leadership of eternal consequence. Over the days I've penned this introduction, my paths again crossed with two longtime friends and ministry colleagues who remind me of this in both words and actions.

Kevin Myers and I have been friends since elementary school. Most people know him for his leadership at 12Stone Church in Atlanta, Georgia, the first church that Kentwood Community Church had a part in helping to launch. But from the vantage point of our friendship, I've glimpsed that his leadership influence emerges from intimacy with the Father; he leads by following. Nothing is more important to Kevin than nurturing this connection through prayer and fasting.

Dennis Jackson, who makes his home in Budapest, Hungary, as European director for Global Partners (missions department of The Wesleyan Church), has been a friend since our days at Marion College. We were best men in each other's weddings. Dennis, whose encouraging and coaching gifts bless the ministries of those serving in Europe, gains the discernment he needs by keeping in step with the Spirit. This connectedness to the Vine helps him and those he works with sense where God is working in the dramatically diverse ministry contexts of Europe.

This following of the Spirit, evidenced in the lives of Kevin and Dennis, is repeatedly displayed in effective leaders, lay and ordained, as they complete the ministry assignments God has given.

As I've studied the life of Joshua in passages that precede the book of Joshua, I've been impressed with what God taught him as a follower of Moses. These lessons, recorded for us in Exodus, Numbers, and Deuteronomy, reveal the story of Joshua's development before the words "Moses my servant is dead" (Josh. 1:2). Spiritual leaders of families, organizations, and churches must be, first and foremost, followers.

This observation of leaders, current and in the pages of Scripture, has led me to envision what I call I^3 (I cubed or I to the third power) servanthood:

- Intimacy: Any lasting fruitfulness is inseparable from being linked to the Vine (John 15:5). As we discern what God is doing and join him in it, we are empowered for service. Fruitfulness and following go hand in hand.
- Intensity: At times, we need to pour out the passion; at other times, we need to exhibit patience. The scriptural pattern of initiating and resting is as old as creation.
- Intentionality: God's greatest work is often the accumulation of little things done faithfully that open the door to more expansive opportunity (Luke 16:10).

In 1996, I wrote the book *Leading When God Is Moving* (re-released as *Ministry Momentum* in 2004). Based on the first four chapters of Joshua, it examined a time when God was directing his people to claim new territory. It was all happening so fast—for Joshua, for the leaders, and for the people. It was one of those times when God graced a movement with the momentum needed to bring dramatic change.

The subsequent book, *Lead On* (2003), picked up with chapter five of Joshua. It's there that the ministry velocity began to change. There was still movement, but it wasn't nearly as dramatic as it had been. God had deliberately determined to ease up on the accelerator so they would learn ministry lessons as they progressed slowly but surely (Ex. 23:29–30).

Combined and updated into *Ministry Velocity*, Joshua's journal unfolds scriptural strategies for sustainable momentum. This resource can be used for personal reflection but may best be explored in community—with other members of a board, ministry team, or small group. Maximizing all the seasons of ministry leads to the vitality and longevity that produce a lifetime of fruitfulness.

1

WHERE DO WE GO FROM HERE?

Joshua 1:1–2

Momentum Builder	Momentum Buster
Momentum is developed by recognizing the need for a new beginning.	Momentum is drained by denying the need for change.

Imagine driving through your community looking for a church that can help fill the nagging void in your life.

You stop at a church near your neighborhood, even though it appears stuck in time. You guess that the church was built sometime in the 1960s, and the last real care it received took place in the 1980s. Unlike most, you decide you'll risk a visit anyway.

Cautiously entering the facility, you can't spot the restrooms, so you assume the wind didn't adversely affect your hair. It seems good that you didn't bring the kids because a passing glance at the nursery makes

> "Those with the greatest vested interest in the present paradigm are least likely to see the new paradigm."
>
> —JOEL BARKER

you doubt that it's safe and clean. When you search for information about the church, all you can find is a rack with some old Sunday school literature and newsletters. They may be meaningful to members, but they don't answer your questions about the church.

> "Forget the former things; do not dwell on the past.
> See, I am doing a new thing! Now it springs up; do you not perceive it?"
> —ISAIAH 43:18-19

You sense the people here love God and know each other well. Some even speak to you; most huddle with their friends. The service begins with music you've never heard, but the singing is enthusiastic. The pastor asks if there are visitors, and you wonder if he will put you on the spot. Fortunately, he appears not to see you (though you suspect you're the only visitor in the place). The message is presented with zeal, and while the pastor appears to be against a lot of things, he doesn't seem quite sure what to do about anything or what the congregation should do. He uses old phrases you haven't heard since your college English literature class and quotes people you've never heard of. He seems sincere, but you have a hard time relating to him. His everyday life seems very different from yours, so he probably wouldn't understand the struggles you're facing.

You're relieved as you depart. Maybe these people have what you are looking for, and maybe you'll visit again. But you're going to try some other churches first—something a bit more your style.

One of the greatest challenges spiritual leaders face is keeping in step with what God is doing today and where he is leading in the future. Dwelling in the past blocks our vision of the new things God is seeking to do (see Isa. 43:18–19). If the past has been wonderful, you can celebrate it and thank God for it. If the past has been abysmal, you can lament it and hope for something better. You can rejoice because of it or grieve over it. But there's one option God doesn't make available—you can never live in the past.

For more than three decades, I've watched the ministries of pastors who are ahead of me a few years, seeking to learn from their experiences. Some of them start brilliantly, reach the peak of their effectiveness early, and then begin the long coast to retirement. Others, while they may begin uneventfully, are always looking for opportunities to grow as persons and pastors. Their ministries gather strength as the years go by, and their best days are still ahead.

As the book of Joshua opens, God is about to open a new chapter in the story of his people. Joshua's ability to provide leadership in this new thing God is doing depends on his willingness to perceive the transition God is bringing about.

READING THE SIGNALS

In the first two verses of Joshua, God signals to his chosen leader that two things are about to change. The first is a change of leadership; the second is a change of location.

"Moses my servant is dead" (Josh. 1:2). That legendary spiritual giant who guided God's people for so many years had gone the way of all mankind. God was doing more than stating the obvious; he was signaling a transition: Moses is dead, new leadership needs to emerge, and Joshua, you're that leader.

"Get ready to cross the Jordan River . . ." (1:2). No more wandering in the desert. The Promised Land, which had only seemed a dream, was about to become a reality. It was time to start moving.

These were more than mundane events—they signaled the new thing God was about to do. Spiritual leaders have the ability to see the hand of God in the happenings of life. Perceiving the signals requires a watchful eye on circumstances plus knowledge of Scripture.

Throughout Scripture, a change in leadership was often the indicator of a new beginning. Sometimes that meant raising up new leaders— Abraham to become the father of a great nation, Joseph to rescue God's people from famine, a prophet to proclaim God's warning to his people, and Paul to spread the gospel throughout the world. At other times, God replaced leadership—David stepped into King Saul's position, Solomon assumed the throne of his father, and Samuel replaced Eli.

Now, Moses was dead. Since God had said Moses would not enter the Promised Land, his death cleared the way for the next movement of God. This signal was amplified by the command to prepare to cross the river. Scriptural accounts of crossing water were often geographical thresholds of change and commitment in a movement of God. The miraculous crossing of the Red Sea was impressed on the mind of every Hebrew, including Joshua. Now it was time to cross another body of water—the Jordan River.

CHURCH TRANSITION SIGNALS

Personal and spiritual growth depends on our ability to see one chapter of life closing and a new one opening. These signals of transition come in different forms—a career change, the loss of a relationship, a physical move, or health issues. They are met with either a desperate attempt to preserve the way things have been, or the recognition that things neither can nor will ever be the same.

This is also true for churches. The ability to perceive the new things God is doing keeps a movement of God fresh and vital. Ignorance or rejection of the signals relegates the best days of a church to the past. What are some of the common signals in the life of a church that things will never be the same?

PASTORAL CHANGE

Like Moses passing the baton to Joshua, so a new chapter in a church's history begins when God provides a new leader. I remember some years ago being contacted by a church asking if I might be interested in serving as their pastor. The church was still fairly young and the founding pastor was leaving. The lay leader who called me said, "We've benefited from the leadership of a Moses. Now we're looking for a Joshua to lead us in the next steps of obedience to the mission God has given us." While I did not accept their invitation, their transition signal was one even I couldn't miss.

Not all pastoral changes are made with a desire to embrace the future. Some pastoral selections are a reaction to a pastor who tried to implement change. The church then looks for someone who won't threaten the status quo. Or the previous pastor had certain strengths and, like all humans, corresponding weaknesses. The church then selects a new pastor whose assets are perceived to compensate for his predecessor's deficits.

I served as a pastor at Kentwood Community Church from its beginning. We started in a unique but effective way: I was the full-time assistant pastor while Dick Wynn, employed as well by Youth for Christ, served as the part-time senior pastor. I'll never forget the day Dick called me into his office to announce that he was accepting a promotion with Youth for Christ and would be moving to their national offices in Wheaton, Illinois. I felt a hollowness in the pit of my stomach as I considered the absence of this man who had been my mentor and had led our church for the first two years of its history (1979–1981). My "Moses" wasn't dead, but he was moving out of town.

Having just celebrated my twenty-fourth birthday, I was now being asked to become the senior pastor. Most of the congregation was supportive while feeling the same nervousness I felt. I'll never forget one reaction though: A former pastor in our congregation told me that he and his wife would be leaving. His explanation? With Dick gone and me as the pastor, they didn't see the church surviving. Now there's a confidence booster!

A pastoral change involves transition. Some in the church will view it positively, some negatively. It is doubtful that all will view it the same way.

FACILITY CHANGES

Our church began in rented facilities. After four months, we moved to a school that we also rented. After another three and a half years, we moved into a facility we had built ourselves and that had a mortgage with our name on it. We were not prepared for what happened next.

We had struggled for nearly four years to assemble a core group for the church. Rented facilities brought numerous inconveniences, such as the lack of classrooms and the lack of control over heating and air conditioning. Almost everyone there believed in the mission and the future of the church; they certainly weren't attracted by the facilities or extensive programs.

Then we opened the doors of the church we had just built. People came, and came, and came. Our attendance doubled in one Sunday. These people didn't know what we believed. We'd made no major changes in our staff or approach to ministry. The only difference was that the facility they had watched being constructed was now completed. Then we learned that in our community, facility equaled credibility. They now took us seriously. We were a "real" church. Their perception of us had changed, and our church would never be the same.

CHANGE OF LAY LEADERSHIP

In many churches, the long-term stability of a congregation is more dependent on a lay leader or small group of lay leaders than on the pastor. Sometimes this stability leads to church health. Other times, it lends to the preservation of the status quo. In these churches, a change in lay leadership can signal the closing of one chapter and opening of the next.

This is particularly true in smaller, rural churches. If a lay leader dies or relocates, the church experiences a period of adjustment. It is also true, though perhaps to a lesser extent, in larger churches. In my church, we have a voluntary rotation system for our board members. The general practice is to serve up to three years and then take at least a year off. Depending on who is rotating off (or on), this change can bring about a new emphasis or direction.

GROWTH BARRIERS

As a church grows, it fundamentally changes. Resistance to these changes by the pastor or the people is the reason most churches plateau. Many of these growth barriers or thresholds have been identified by researchers like Carl George and Warren Bird, authors of the book *How to Break Growth Barriers*.[1] There are certain predictable transitions that come as a church enlarges numerically.

Like most pastors, one of the toughest transitions for me was the two hundred barrier. During the first four years of our church's existence, I knew almost everyone, and everyone knew me. I had coffee in their homes; I could name their kids; I knew where they worked and the hobbies they enjoyed. When we moved into our new building, I found myself speaking to a sea of unrecognizable faces. I was on cloud nine because of the outreach taking place, but I struggled with my inability to personally minister to everyone.

While this was mostly a secret struggle, I shared my feelings on one occasion with a dear older saint in our church. As I sat in her home enjoying one of her delicious homemade cookies, I bemoaned the fact I couldn't visit with everyone who was coming to church. She very lovingly assured me that she and others would miss those fairly frequent visits as well. Then she said something I'll never forget: "Wayne, we love you, and it's good to get to know you. But it's just more important that people get to know Jesus than get to know you."

The Holy Spirit brought those words home to my heart with conviction. Would I limit what God was doing to my personal comfort zone, or would I adjust my comfort zone to be in step with him? That day, I made a commitment I've needed to revisit many times since—that bearing my cross means obeying God, even if it's uncomfortable.

In *Growing Plans*, Lyle Schaller identifies and illustrates how a church changes as it grows.[2] He makes clear what so many church leaders have learned: A growing church is a changing church. A large church is not an overgrown small church. Its life is governed by a fundamentally different set of principles.

COMMUNITY CHANGES

Not only do churches change, but communities do as well. If a major employer moves out of or into a community, a church is impacted. If the ethnic or economic demographics of a community change, the effectiveness of a church's outreach is altered. If a rural community is absorbed in the urban sprawl of a metropolitan area, expectations for a church's ministry change.

Kentwood Community Church was committed to parenting new churches. We particularly targeted outlying communities in the greater Grand Rapids, Michigan area. These communities were not only growing as Grand Rapids grew, but they were changing. The people moving in were no longer farmers but commuters who worked in the city. The churches that traditionally existed in the communities continued to be effective in ministering to long-term residents but struggled to meet the needs of the changing population. These new residents had different social and spiritual needs. Often, a new church meets such needs best, but many existing churches are learning to broaden their ministries to include a wider variety of people.

These are but a few of the transition times churches may face. Some transitions are the result of conscious decisions a church has made, such as offering multiple services, adjusting worship styles, or providing pastoral care through small groups. Others are the result of factors beyond the control of church leaders. Like Joshua, they must adjust to the realities of external conditions over which they exercise little control.

SENSING THE LOSS

There is a myth that keeps many spiritual leaders from taking action when God's Spirit prompts them. The myth is this: If it is God's will, everyone will feel good about it. In reality, the first feeling that comes with most substantive transitions is a sense of loss, and then a tendency to resist that change. In fact, scholars who study change dynamics have concluded that if there is no sense of loss and there is no resistance, then there has been no real change.

So every change involves a sense of loss, even when we are excited about it. When a chapter in a person's life or a local church closes, a grief process takes place. If we could peer into Joshua's journal, I'm convinced we would find that he was experiencing the whirlwind of emotions that comes with letting go of the past.

LOSS OF IDENTITY

Like many men, Joshua's role was part of what defined him. He had been known for years as Moses' aide. His relationship with Moses had given Joshua his identity. Now, Moses was gone.

Moses had been Joshua's spiritual director and mentor. They had shared many significant spiritual moments together:

- They had fought battles together. Joshua had wielded a sword in physical battle while he saw Moses with hands lifted high carrying on the spiritual battle (Ex. 17:8–16). On that day, Joshua undoubtedly learned that the battles he would fight in the future would be so much more than struggles with flesh and blood; they would require prayer and dependence on God.
- Joshua had been trusted by Moses with a special assignment to explore the Promised Land (Num. 13–14). Joshua and Caleb had encouraged Moses and the people of Israel with the challenge that they could take the land.
- Joshua had defended Moses' right to lead the people and speak for God (Num. 11:26–30). Moses had taught him that not all spiritual authority and blessings were confined to the leader God had chosen.
- Joshua had been present during many of Moses' intimate encounters with God (Ex. 33–34).

Joshua was an aide to a great spiritual leader. No one was nor ever would be like Moses, even in God's eyes (Deut. 34:10–12). Joshua would never again be able to ask him questions, watch his actions, or seek his prayers.

A friend once shared with me his difficulty in adjusting to the death of his father. His sense of loss was amplified when he called his father's home not long after the funeral. With all the activity that had taken place, no one had thought to change the message on the answering machine. He heard his father's voice saying, "I'm not available to take your call right now." He realized in that moment that his dad would never be available to take his calls. An incredible feeling of loneliness and loss overtook him. Joshua must have felt the same. Moses was no longer personally available to respond to him.

LOSS OF FAMILIARITY

"Now then . . . cross the Jordan River into the land I am about to give to them—to the Israelites" (Josh. 1:2). The Israelites were about to fulfill the dream God had given them decades before, but they were also leaving the only way of life they had ever known. This generation had grown up in the desert. They were familiar with the ways of the desert, while that which was to come would be new territory.

Think of the maintenance mentality that must have developed during those desert wanderings. The parents and grandparents must have continually shared stories about the good old days. Undoubtedly the story of the ten plagues and the crossing of the Red Sea were fireside favorites. They told the stories of a movement of God, but this new generation had never experienced a movement of God first-hand. They had a second-hand faith and forty years in maintenance mode, while God disposed of their unfaithful forefathers.

Adopting a consumer mentality, their lives centered on their needs. They approached God with a feed-me mindset, expecting manna from heaven and then complaining about it when it arrived. When their needs were not met, their consumerism led them to whine to each other and question the authority of their leaders—even the great Moses.

Stuck in a rut and focused on their needs—that description fits many churches today.

Joshua was called to lead the Israelites into unfamiliar territory. They wanted guarantees he couldn't give. They wanted to know exactly what this new land was like, how they would get their food, and what would be expected of them. These were questions he could not completely answer, since he had only briefly visited the territory decades earlier. He wasn't familiar with the challenges they would face in that land now. They could only meet them as they faced them together. They would have to exercise faith, which, by definition, means moving beyond the familiar.

It's precisely at this point that many churches experience what Robert Dale labels nostalgia or organizational homesickness. In his book *To Dream Again*, he observes that the word *nostalgia* is derived from two Greek words meaning "to return home" and "a painful condition."[3] Change can prompt wistful longings in all of us. When movements of God are between chapters, the future can seem threatening and the past attractive. This causes some tentativeness. As a temporary condition, it is fairly harmless and normal.

The loss of the familiar, even when the familiar is a result of disobedience to God, is still a loss. I've been with families who wanted to structure an intervention to confront an alcoholic family member. Their sincere desire was to see a change in that person. I've also watched those same families undercut that person's attempt to change when they recognized their lives would be different as well. The present was dysfunctional, even sinful, but it was familiar.

All that was happening to Joshua and Israel was God's will, but taking hold of the future would mean letting go of the past. There's a certain amount of grieving that's normal anytime God brings about change in the life of a person or a church. The process looks like this:

- Step 1: Denial. The focus is on the past. Nothing needs to change. Problems will go away. Effort is given to preserve things as they have been.
- Step 2: Discomfort. There are changes taking place. Things will never be the same. Resistance to these changes and anger about them are typical reactions.
- Step 3: Discovery. There is a willingness to begin to explore the future. The next step is unclear and unfamiliar, but possible opportunities begin to emerge.
- Step 4: Devotion. Commitment emerges to act upon a new vision of the future.

Spiritual leaders realize that change, even when it is God's will, is a process. Not everyone may feel good about it. Many times the first reaction to God's conviction is one of denial and discomfort. He persists in the process until his people adjust to his plans for them.

Leaders need to show the same kind of persistence. If people react hesitantly to a future vision, is that a sign it's not of God? Not necessarily. Is it a sign the people aren't spiritual? Not necessarily. It's a sign that we're human and that change means the loss of the way things are in order to prepare for the way God wants them to be.

PREPARING TO MOVE ON

"Now then, you and all these people, get ready" (1:2). As you're closing one chapter, begin preparing for the transition into the next chapter. Don't forget the lessons of the past, but prepare to move beyond past patterns and experiences.

This transition time would have been a double whammy for Joshua. At the same time he was working through a loss, he needed to learn new skills. He was no longer the assistant but the leader. The people were no longer desert nomads but a conquering army. They had one foot in history while stepping with the other foot toward a new opportunity. One chapter rarely closes completely before the next starts to open. Transition means uncomfortably straddling chapters for awhile.

Preparing to move on with God is somewhat different for each person or church, but the following guidelines may help to prepare for the transition.

ACKNOWLEDGE THE LOSS

Anyone familiar with the grieving process knows that it varies for each person. It's impossible to predict the exact emotions we will feel or the time it will take to work through them. But one thing is certain—we may resist the grieving process or welcome it, but we will go through it.

When making the transition from one chapter to the next, the degree of loss depends on how much the previous chapter was valued and how much excitement the next one holds. If someone has derived great value and pleasure from the previous chapter, the loss will be intense. If someone is glad to close that previous chapter so they can move into an intriguing and exciting next chapter, the sense of loss is minimized.

The challenge is that people tend to value chapters of life differently. Think for a moment of a married couple. The husband may find it very difficult to change chapters in his career—most men receive much of their identity from their careers. The wife, on the other hand, may find it very difficult to change chapters at home. He may not understand why an impending empty nest bothers her so much, while she may view his reaction to a change in job responsibilities as being too extreme. That's why times of transition call for increased communication and understanding in a marriage.

The same is true for a church. When we're finding it difficult to see eye-to-eye at our church, we talk about not being on the same page. In reality, sometimes we are not in the same chapter. Church members often have an emotional investment in different chapters of a church's history. So, each member may react to change a little differently. Increased communication and understanding, rather than impatience and avoidance of the issue, will allow people to grieve over the past so they can move into the future.

PROCESS CHANGE AT YOUR SPEED

How we process change is influenced by more than the sense of loss we experience. It is influenced by our personality. Some people gain a sense of security from the past while others are continually pursuing the next big challenge. Some latch on to the big picture and are invigorated by pursuing the unexplored, while others have an eye for detail and are interested only in the next step.

The speed at which we process a change is also influenced by whether we believe we've had a choice in the change. Resistance is much greater when we feel a change has been forced upon us. The more we're part of the process of change and have had a voice in shaping the next chapter, the more ready we'll be to welcome what is coming next.

Another factor is our past experience with change. If we have had to make very few changes in job or family situations, any change seems imposing because we've had little opportunity to manage change previously. On the other end of the continuum, if we feel our whole life is one change after another, we may feel overwhelmed and may long for one area of life to remain the same. Our change overload at work and home may lead us to defend the way things are at church, so that we can have a secure sanctuary in a changing world.

The speed at which we process change is influenced by all of these factors. It is true for every person in a church. Understanding these factors will create some freedom for people to make transitions at their pace.

DON'T GET STUCK BETWEEN CHAPTERS

While each of us has the right to process change at our own speed, we do not have the right to stop the process. Any healthy grieving process ultimately involves moving beyond the sense of loss over the way things were and into active pursuit of the way God wants them to be.

Transition times tend to make or break individuals. Harbored anger or a root of bitterness causes us to miss out on God's grace (Heb. 12:15). Prolonged pity parties drain us of the strength and vision to pursue the future work God desires us to do in life. A choice must be made to move on. That choice may be rooted in desire or personal fulfillment, or it may come out of a sense of responsibility to our relationship with God and with others. Feelings need to be acknowledged but not enthroned. Joshua may have felt that Moses' death couldn't have come at a worse time—right when they needed to conquer enemy forces and acquire the Promised Land. But Joshua also knew that God expected him to "get ready to cross the Jordan River into the land" (Josh. 1:2).

Transition times also make or break churches. Many churches are stuck between chapters, dwelling in the past and hesitating about the future. The felt needs of the members carry greater weight than a commitment to obedience. God patiently allows churches to adjust to change, but he also expects spiritual leaders to prepare for the next chapter of his great redemptive story that is about to unfold.

WATCH YOUR FOCUS

Yes, Joshua, Moses is dead, but God is alive and well. Resist the tendency to become absorbed in your emotions or to react to the feelings of others. A vertical focus is essential. Keep one eye on what is happening to you and the other eye on what God is doing in you.

Getting ready to move on to what God is doing means listening to him. It involves knowing what God has done through his Word and your personal experiences and also what God will do for you and his people in the days ahead.

ANTICIPATING THE FUTURE

God began his conversation with Joshua by looking back: "Moses my servant is dead." He continued it by sharing with him what needed to take place: "Get ready" (Josh. 1:2). He acknowledged past realities and defined the present action step, then shifted the focus to the future: Prepare to enter "into the land I am about to give to them—to the Israelites" (1:2). Start anticipating what is yet to come.

Anticipating the future does not mean rejecting the past, but rather learning from it so that we can move forward. Like rowing a boat, we face backward only to more effectively move forward. We look back not because that is the direction we are intending to go, but because it maximizes our strength and gives us reference points in moving ahead.

One of the great joys God grants us is anticipation. Sometimes anticipation exceeds reality. Anticipating a vacation may be better than the vacation itself. Looking forward to retirement may be better than living in retirement. Dreaming about owning a business may be more hassle-free than being the actual owner.

The Christian life is one of anticipation. We look forward to God's answers to our prayers. We seek to discover his will for our lives, knowing that our stewardship of time, abilities, and money has eternal consequences. By faith, we believe all the injustices of human existence will eventually be addressed and that eternity will reveal the reward of faithful service to our heavenly Father. We know the final reality of heaven will exceed any of our anticipation.

Anticipating our final destination may be easier than anticipating the next step God has for us as we journey with him. Like Joshua, we know there will be thresholds of commitment to cross, battles to be waged, and comfort zones to be stretched. God will do his part, but he expects us to obediently complete our part as well.

While transition begins with the loss experienced in closing a chapter of life, it reaches its fruition in the anticipation of opening a new chapter. These times of change create opportunities for greater dependence upon God and greater openness to his plan for us. Spiritual leaders and churches also need to welcome these chapter changes, anticipating the blessing of experiencing firsthand a participation in a movement of God.

2

DISCOVERING GOD'S NEW FRONTIER

Joshua 1:3–5

Momentum Builder	**Momentum Buster**
Momentum is developed by creating a clear and focused vision statement.	Momentum is drained by shooting at nothing or attempting to do everything.

We see them every day at work, in our neighborhood, even at church—people who drag through life day in, day out, year after repetitive year. People are grinding away their lives and spending their time on tasks that fail to challenge their souls. They seem sedated by the monotony of a life that is too small for the breath of God that is within them. Their spirits long for a movement of God to envelop their inner being and give them purpose for living.

Over time, apathy and negativism develop. In the words of Price Pritchett, "Unable to make any promising connection between a troubled

> "The place where God calls you is where your deep gladness and the world's deep hunger intersect."
> —FREDERICK BUECHNER

today and a vague tomorrow, they fall into a weary pattern of doubt, cynicism, and disillusionment."[1] Maybe that's why we live in a society that places so little hope and trust in government, schools, or the church. Maybe that's why God is raising up spiritual leaders who live their lives on purpose and lead their churches to do the same.

> "May he remember all your sacrifices and accept your burnt offerings. May he give you the desire of your heart and make all your plans succeed."
> —PSALM 20:3–4

Joshua knew that God was opening a new chapter in the life of his people. While sensing the loss of the way things were, he knew he could not back into the future. He knew he must look forward to God's purpose for the days ahead. This purpose is pointedly revealed in Joshua 1:3–5. A closer look at these verses provides a lesson for spiritual leaders in the indispensable dimensions of a God-given vision.

SEEK THE OPPORTUNITIES

The best opportunities are those that fulfill the promises of God. God tells Joshua, "I will give you every place where you set your foot, as I promised Moses. Your territory will extend" (1:3–4). God is unveiling a glimpse of the opportunities that lie ahead. It's just God and Joshua, alone in conversation about the future God has prepared.

I have been an avid reader of what is taking place in churches around our nation. I have often visited churches that are a bit ahead of my own church in their development or in a particular area of ministry. I have called other pastors to ask them what they are doing. I surveyed our congregation and talked with our leadership teams. But I am convinced that, apart from time alone with God, all of those activities are futile. It is persistence in prayer that will move a church's ministry plan beyond mimicking what others are doing to fulfill God's unique promises to its leaders.

We are created in the image of God. That gives us the ability to be creative, to see that which is unseen. We not only can sense the future, but have a role in creating it. This capacity is part of the created order, God's design for humanity. It even works apart from God. Many people with no allegiance to God accomplish great things by thinking of possibilities and visualizing the future. But God seeks to sanctify that creative capacity so that the possibilities envisioned are based on his promises and aligned with his purposes.

While it would be wonderful to think that vision is a characteristic most plentifully found among the people of God, many churches fail to seek God-promised opportunities. Joshua and the Israelites were not naturally inclined to envision the future because of the blinders they were wearing. Which of the blinders present in their lives then are found among churches today?

THEY WANDERED WITHOUT A SPECIFIC DIRECTION FOR A LONG TIME

The Israelites spent forty years marking time as shepherds in the desert. It was the fulfillment of God's declaration to the previous generation: "Your children will be shepherds here for forty years . . . one year for each of the forty days you explored the land—you will suffer for your sins and know what it is like to have me against you" (Num. 14:33–34). The people whom Joshua would lead into the Promised Land had lived their whole lives meandering in a wasteland.

Many churches have a history of wandering. They mark time by doing the same thing they have always done, not pursuing any specific direction. This makes it challenging to think clearly and specifically about future opportunities.

THEY DEVELOPED A MANNA MENTALITY

During their time in the desert, God miraculously provided the Israelites' daily sustenance. Moses spent his time responding to their complaints about the menu. In their minds, leadership existed for the purpose of meeting their needs.

Don't miss this blinder. Many Christians cannot envision anything beyond their needs. There is a world of difference between believing that the purpose of leadership is to meet our needs and believing that the purpose of leadership is to help us conquer new territory in obedience to God. God will not do great things through people whose only expectation of leadership is to have their needs met. He can do great things through people who expect leaders to conquer new territory. As a church ages, there is a tendency for the focus to move from reaching the community (taking new territory) to catering to the preferences of the members (meet our needs). Maybe that's why most churches reach their peak before they are two decades old.

I saw this tendency at Kentwood Community Church—and in my life. When our church started, we had to take new territory for God. If we hadn't, we would not have survived. As time passed, it was so tempting to make our top priority meeting the needs of people who faithfully attended, served, and gave. We began to judge the value of every worship service by what we got out of it instead of asking whether it was challenging to someone who did not yet know Christ. There is nothing wrong with having one's spiritual needs met. But there is a balance between meeting needs and taking new territory. A movement of God requires us to transcend self-centeredness to extend his kingdom.

THEY TRIED WHAT JOSHUA ENVISIONED AND FAILED

Because of the Israelites' unbelief, God sentenced a whole generation to die in the desert. Unhappy with God's decision, they tried to take matters into their own hands and enter the Promised Land. "Nevertheless, in their presumption they went up toward the high hill country, though neither Moses nor the ark of the LORD's covenant moved from the camp. Then the Amalekites and Canaanites who lived in that hill country came down and attacked them and beat them down all the way to Hormah" (Num. 14:44–45). Their defeat came as they belatedly tried to do what was no longer God's will. They attempted to conquer new territory in their own strength and without God's resources.

So many times the comment is made, "That's been tried before, and it didn't work." It may be a reference to a past ministry initiative, fund-raising campaign, or building program. A failure of the past limits opportunities for the future. The vision God gave Joshua was no different from the one he'd given Moses: enter the Promised Land. But a closer look reveals the most important difference of all—that this time the movement was God's will and he would provide the victory. It was the same task, but a new leader, new followers, and a renewed commitment from God.

THEY SUFFERED FOR THE UNFAITHFULNESS OF THEIR FOREFATHERS

Joshua wandered in the desert for forty years not because of his lack of vision or obedience, but because he was outvoted by ten other spies. The generation he was to lead into the Promised Land had not shared in the disobedient actions that brought about their desert experience. God predicted it when he announced, "Your children will be shepherds here for forty years, suffering for *your* unfaithfulness" (Num. 14:33, emphasis added).

It's tough when you have to suffer for your sins. It's even tougher when you suffer because others have been unfaithful to God. I see it in the lives of individuals who have experienced abuse, been impacted by divorce, or unjustly treated at work. There is a tremendous temptation to be bitter, which always magnifies the past and clouds the future. I have seen it in the lives of churches when past leaders did not take the necessary steps of faith. They become mired in the should-have-beens and could-have-beens, completely missing what yet could be by the grace of God.

Courageous spiritual leaders won't allow the blinders of past experiences to block their vision of God-given opportunities. In times of prayer, God reveals our blinders and challenges our self-centeredness or self-pity. He encourages us to step out and take new territory in our spiritual lives and in the mission of our church. The experience of personal and public worship frees us to long for what

God promises to provide. It is no mistake that when the psalmist says, "May [the Lord] give you the desire of your heart and make all your plans succeed" (Ps. 20:4), the verse immediately preceding it says, "May he remember all your sacrifices and accept your burnt offerings" (Ps. 20:3). Your worship (sacrifices) and self-denial (offerings) position you to seek the opportunities.

SEE THE BOUNDARIES

God promises Joshua, "I will give you every place where you set your foot" (Josh. 1:3). But God also limits where Joshua will set his feet—the extent of the property. "Your territory will extend from the desert to Lebanon, and from the great river, the Euphrates—all the Hittite country—to the Great Sea on the west" (1:4). Those are the boundaries—the desert, Lebanon, Euphrates, and the Great Sea.

A God-given vision includes not only the possibilities, but also the boundaries. We are created in the image of God, so we can sense the opportunities. Yet we are creatures, restricted by time and space. Like all creatures, there are limits to what can be done by one individual or one church. Limits can be resisted or they can be appreciated—but they are real.

I grew up in a small Wesleyan church. I remember hearing about large churches, though they were not common. I also remember pastors saying, "If we were a big church, we could . . ." Maybe that's why I came to believe that a big church could do it all. What a myth! Later, I had the responsibility of leading a church that fit my earlier definition of big. Yet I learned that larger churches still struggle with the limitations of money, facility, and personnel. A church never gets to the place where it can offer an endless smorgasbord of ministry opportunities. There will always be a need to set priorities and postpone some ministries to another day.

A clear vision statement includes not only what a church will say yes to, but what it will say no to as well. The ideal would be a statement with such great clarity that church leaders could use it as a filter with confidence. It would help them to say, "Yes, we'll be involved in that," but also to say, "While that ministry may be valuable, it doesn't fit within the territory God has promised to us."

Learning to say no is one of the toughest tasks of spiritual leaders. I remember as a young pastor hearing the late Dr. Orval Butcher say, "The problem with most Wesleyan churches is not who we are willing to win, but who we're not willing to lose." It was his way of saying he'd seen churches completely lose their vision and momentum in an attempt to appease one powerful person or interest group in the church. Attempts to please all the people or meet every need drain energy that might otherwise be focused on moving the vision forward.

Boundaries are like the banks of a river. Banks create depth and increase the momentum of the water as it flows. Rivers without banks are slow and shallow. Churches without boundaries in their vision statements try to please everyone, do everything, and embrace the latest fad. The result is ministry that can be described as a mile wide and an inch deep.

What makes it tough to say no is the tension it creates. Everybody gets excited about what can be done, but since Adam and Eve, we've struggled with our creaturely limits. That struggle is intensified by living in a world that deceptively promises we can have it all. I've seen it in our church planting efforts. We bring in a church planter who begins to share his vision with a core group of people. This process is sometimes referred to as an agenda agreement. The core group may be excited to hear, for instance, that small groups will be a major emphasis in the life of that new church. Pastoral care will be given by the group leader and other members of the group. But what will happen the first time one of those individuals is hospitalized, and the small group leader visits, but the pastor doesn't? Is pastoral care through small groups still a great idea? It is often when something is not done that the true implications of a vision become clear.

A few years ago, I visited several newer and smaller churches in the Grand Rapids area. I was surprised by the number of people who had formerly attended our church and who were now part of these new churches. Sitting in the back of one church, I could identify by name twenty-seven of the sixty-three people in the auditorium. I conducted some spontaneous exit interviews, asking why they had chosen to leave our church. Several reasons were mentioned, but most often it was that the church is just too big. I asked if they had been part of a small group or class, and most of them had not. But even those who had, expressed a desire to be part of a church where they recognized most of the faces in the worship services and could rather spontaneously spend time with the pastor. I left wanting to meet that need, but painfully recognized I had encountered one of the boundaries of a larger church ministry. Large churches have limits; small churches have limits. A clear vision acknowledges those limits.

Sometimes a vision dictates that the answer be, "No, it will never happen." As uncomfortable as it might be for me, our church will never be one big, happy family. It's impossible to even get everyone in the sanctuary at the same time, let alone know everyone who is there. We are a church with many families—small groups, classes, and special ministries. When we gather to worship, it is a family reunion—a gathering of family groups related by the blood of Christ.

At other times, the vision dictates, "No, we cannot do it at this time." I call this the principle of uneven development. It's a myth to believe that a church develops its ministry simultaneously and equally on all fronts. I've witnessed this in our building programs. The first facility on our present site rather equally served the various ministry areas. Due to the rapid growth of attendance but a more limited growth in finances, our next addition increased space for children's and youth ministries but did nothing to relieve overcrowding in worship. So, we added additional services. When designing our new sanctuary, we addressed our need for nursery and worship space but had to postpone adding another educational wing and offices. We have told our congregation all along that no one building program will ever meet all our needs. Finances or facilities cause temporary limits. Sometimes those limits relate to time or volunteers. The need fits within the framework of our vision, but not within our present resources.

Every time church leaders say yes or no, the vision becomes clearer. That's why vision statements must be living, open to revision. The process of thinking through a vision is even more valuable than what ends up on paper. It's the exercise of listening to God, examining present realities and strategically considering the future that God uses to reveal his will to his people.

SET THE TERRITORIES

When God promised Joshua to give him the land he was walking on, victory came day by day, one step at a time. He did not take all of the territory at once. He experienced small successes on the way to embracing all that God had shown him. There were territories within the Promised Land that were eventually divided among the twelve tribes of Israel.

Spiritual leaders establish territories within their personal life mission statement. I'm convinced spiritual leaders should be accountable for goals in the various arenas of life. Among them are:

- Personal: maintaining a level of physical fitness, stretching their minds and opening their hearts to share more of themselves with others.
- Relational: allotting time and energy for their spouses, children, and deepening relationships so they develop beyond acquaintances to true friendships.
- Spiritual: exercising the spiritual disciplines of time spent in God's Word, prayer, Scripture memory, journaling, and fasting.
- Vocational: honoring God with all of their work, whether paid or volunteer, constantly striving to produce lasting results.
- Financial: learning to be good stewards as they earn, give, save, and enjoy what God has entrusted to them.

I find it helpful to periodically review the current priority each area holds in my life as evidenced in my actions, checkbook, and calendar. I then recommit these territories to the desired priority level.

In a similar way, churches should identify in their vision statement territories God has promised them. In our vision statement, we called these key result areas. Let me illustrate by sharing the vision statement we developed for Kentwood Community Church (subject to continual refinement).[2] There were three stanzas to it—one for attenders (KCCers), one for the unchurched or de-churched around us (community), and one for missions (world):

> **For Every KCCer:** Activating steps of personal maturity in Christ within a large church family through holistic ministry.
>
> **For Our Community:** Initiating opportunities for every home in the area to experience the redemptive life of Christ through active church involvement.
>
> **For Our World:** Engaging in strategic regional, national, and international outreach through partnership with other organizations.

Our vision statement was an attempt to succinctly express our strategy for impacting people for Christ. It did not stand alone but was based on our mission statement. Our mission statement expressed the biblical foundation for our ministry: To glorify God through active worship, empowering God's people for new levels of redemptive living and service, and building God's kingdom through thoughtful and creative communication of the changeless truth of Jesus Christ to a world that will never be the same.

Our mission statement was a brief synopsis of our theology of ministry; our vision statement was a brief synopsis of our strategy for ministry. Out of our vision came five territories of ministry—our key result areas.

RELATIONSHIP NETWORKS

This first key result area expressed our commitment to help people care for one another by being in relationships with each other. It drove our attempts to multiply the number of our small groups and ensured there was a dimension of fellowship to our classes. As a large church, we knew that a sense of community would not be generated by knowing everyone. We taught our new members about four levels of fellowship:

Celebration. Worship times were designed to help us fellowship with God. These were intended to create intimacy with God but allow a level of anonymity with other people.

Connections. These were class settings that varied in size from fifteen to one hundred fifty people. They were centered on instruction, but opportunity was provided to share names and prayer requests.

C.A.R.E. Caring About Reaching Everyone was the theme of our small group ministry. Varying in size from three to twenty people, the goal was to share life experiences and build spiritual depth through caring and praying for each other.

Covenant. These were one-on-one relationships (or groups of three) for the purpose of accountability. Meetings were based on a covenant to accomplish specific, tangible goals to achieve personal and spiritual growth.

Relationship networks sometimes began during a worship time, but they never developed there. It was in Connections, C.A.R.E. groups, and Covenant partnerships that true fellowship was enriched.

DEVELOPMENT OF PERSONAL GIFTEDNESS

Every believer is gifted by God for ministry. Lay ministers are most effective and most fulfilled when using their spiritual gifts in an area of service where they have a God-given passion.

BIBLICAL COMPREHENSION AND APPLICATION

Alarmed by the level of biblical illiteracy present even among believers, we committed ourselves to helping people discover the whole counsel of God and apply it to their everyday lives.

OUTREACH TO AREA HOMES

As expressed in our vision statement, we took the initiative to introduce people to the redemptive life of Christ. We did not passively wait for them to come to us, but we actively built bridges to reach out to them. The focus of our strategy for evangelism was not on media or crusades, although we occasionally utilized those means. It was to enfold people into the church.

PARTNERSHIPS FOR MISSIONS

We partnered with other organizations and people to most effectively reach our nation and world.

These five territories of ministry were reflected in the specific annual goals of every department of our church. Two things took place on a regular basis. First, we monitored each key result area to ensure it was being lived out in the life of our church. If there was ever a time when one of these results was not being pursued, we were being unfaithful to our mission. By definition, a key result area was to be continually practiced and never neglected. Second, we ranked these key result areas each year in order of priority. The one at the top of the list was our number one priority for that given year; the one on the bottom of the list was the lowest priority for that year. Again, all of them had to take place each year, but the amount of attention given to each varied from year to year depending on the opportunities that were present. For instance, when we were building a new sanctuary, our number one key result area was relationship networks. We concentrated on building a strong fellowship base within the church. Our lowest key result area at the time was outreach to area homes, in part due to the limitations of our facilities. When we moved into our new sanctuary, we made outreach to area homes our number one key result area. This was a window of opportunity to make a significant impact on our community. And by that time, we had developed relationship networks to help newcomers sense the warmth of our fellowship.

We tentatively projected five years in advance the annual ranking of our key result areas. They were subject to change as we got closer to the actual year, but it helped us maintain a long-term perspective on our short-term strategy.

Into what territories is God leading your church? What results are necessary for you to be faithful to the vision God is giving you?

DEVELOP YOUR VISION FOR MINISTRY

If you've never attempted to create a written vision statement for your church, what I've shared may seem overwhelming and complex. Our vision statement was generated over a period of years and had enough detail to be sure all our staff and lay leaders were moving forward in the same direction. Your statement may be very different from ours, or it may be similar. The important thing is that it says what you sense God is saying to you.

Developing a vision is a process. In my life and at Kentwood Community Church, the development of our original vision statement took place in this way. First, I devoted considerable time to reading about vision. There are many excellent resources available from authors like Aubrey Malphurs, C. Peter Wagner, Bob Logan, and George Barna. One of the briefest descriptions of the perspectives to be included in vision is by Warren Bennis and Burt Nanus in their book *Leaders*.[3] They highlight the following dimensions:

- Foresight: to judge how the vision fits with the way the environment of the organization may evolve.
- Hindsight: so that the vision does not violate the traditions and culture of the organization.
- World View: within which to determine the impact of possible new developments and trends.
- Depth Perception: so that the whole picture can be seen in appropriate detail and perspective.
- Peripheral Vision: so that possible responses of competitors and other stakeholders to the new direction can be comprehended.
- Revision: so that all visions previously synthesized are constantly reviewed as the environment changes.

While these insights come from a secular book, I found it helpful to ask God for each of these dimensions of vision as I attempted to see our future.

Second, I devoted concentrated time to prayer. I asked God to allow me to see things as he does and to know what new territory he wanted our church to conquer. During these times, I attempted to write a description of our church ten years from now, including people being reached, size, how lives were being changed, ministries that were being offered, facilities that had been built, and so on.

Next, I created a rough draft of our vision statement. Up to this point, the process of vision development had been just between God and me. Now, I created something to which other leaders in our church could respond. Every copy was labeled "rough draft" to indicate the vision statement was in process and that other input would be welcome.

Fourth, in meetings with our staff, church board, and other lay leaders, we refined the vision statement. In most areas, there was give and take, though in some areas, I held firmly to the original draft. I found myself feeling a bit defensive, since I had already spent so much time with the statement. But I realized that the refinements suggested by others allowed for their ownership of the final statement.

Fifth, it was presented to various groups within our church for their reaction and input. While by this time we were not making major revisions, their suggestions did serve to fine-tune our vision and expose some of the blind spots.

Finally, it was presented to the whole congregation for formal adoption. By this time, nearly every leader in our church had seen it and been given an opportunity to respond to it. The final adoption was more of a ceremonial event.

The first time we created a vision statement, the whole process took about ten months. Steps one, two, and three occurred rather simultaneously and took two to three months. Step four took an additional four months. Steps five and six took about three months. The length of the process depends on factors such as previous experience, the size of the church, the degree of unity among leaders, and the credibility of the pastor and church board. Remember, it is the process that's valuable, not just the final product. Don't rush it, but don't let it bog down. And every step of the way, listen to what God is promising you.

REMEMBER THAT GOD KEEPS HIS PROMISES

A vision from God involves more than the promise of results (Josh. 1:3–4). It is centered on a relationship with him (1:5). God promised Joshua that he would never be alone as the Israelites pursued the conquest of the Promised Land.

God never promised Joshua that it would be easy—in fact he talked to him about the need for courage. He did not promise conflict-free conquest—there would be many battles and setbacks before Joshua's conquest was over. And God did not promise an immediate conquest—it would take years for the territory to be taken.

God did promise significant results (from his perspective) and a relationship that would prove he is faithful and available every step of the way. God promised Joshua that he wouldn't have to go alone. No matter how challenging it became, God would be there. And he will be there for you too.

3

COURAGE THAT COUNTS

Joshua 1:6-9

Momentum Builder	**Momentum Buster**
Momentum is developed by having the strength and courage to act upon God's will.	Momentum is drained by remaining in our comfort zones rather than following our convictions.

Imagine a blossoming courtship between a young man and a young woman. As their relationship begins, they are cautious about sharing too much of their hearts until they know each other better. As time goes on and they enjoy each other's company, they begin to reveal more of themselves. They may even begin to look to the future, dreaming about what it would be like to spend the rest of their lives together.

Up to this point, their future has been a matter of conversation and imagination. If the relationship is to last, there will come a time when they ponder their commitment to each other. They will ask themselves,

> "Success is never final. Failure is never fatal.
> It is courage that counts."
>
> —WINSTON CHURCHILL

"Will I give myself only to this person—for better, for worse, for richer, for poorer, as long as we both shall live?"

> "Be on your guard; stand firm in the faith; be men of courage; be strong."
> —1 CORINTHIANS 16:13

The first few verses of Joshua allow us to eavesdrop on a conversation between God and his newly appointed leader. A movement of God begins with a person who is willing to listen to the purposes of a sovereign God for his people. Up to this point, everything that has been communicated has been just between God and Joshua.

That's about to change. Soon Joshua would go public and announce God's vision for the days ahead. He would begin to challenge other leaders and prepare the people to move into the Promised Land. It was time for a gut check—an internal test to be certain Joshua had the commitment to pursue the vision, for better, for worse, for richer, for poorer. Was the vision of God he had received simply a good idea, or would he obey God every step of the way until it became a reality?

In the days ahead, there would be few tangible rewards for this new leader. The only thing that would keep the vision alive, from a human perspective, would be the leader's faith and commitment. Getting this movement off the ground would require constant attention to problems not previously encountered. In a word, it would require *courage*. And that's exactly what God addressed in Joshua 1:6–9.

COURAGE FOR INFLUENCE

"Be strong and courageous, because you will *lead* these people" (1:6, emphasis added). Joshua had been Moses' aide, but now he was the point person in a fresh movement of God. We don't need great courage to be influenced by others. We must be strong and courageous if we intend to influence others.

God knew that if Joshua provided lukewarm leadership, this movement wouldn't make it into the Promised Land. There are many good ideas and great dreams, and there are many people who hear God whisper his intentions for their lives. But without a passionate investment of energy and influence, they will never conquer new territory.

I'm convinced that spiritual leaders and churches that are growing aren't more creative than those that aren't growing. And they may not be more spiritual. What is the difference? It is the courage to act upon what God shows them—to be an influence rather than to simply respond to the random requests of those around them.

- That courage is seen in a pastor who prayerfully seeks God's priorities for ministry, and who is not deterred from acting upon those priorities by distracting demands.
- It is seen in the members of a church board that envision the ministry God has for their church and make that ministry the centerpiece of their monthly agenda, rather than dwelling on a disgruntled member or the latest problem with the building.
- This courage is seen in a church that does not allow its ministry to degenerate into responding only to the concerns of those within its walls, but seeks to permeate the surrounding community with the good news of Jesus Christ.
- God looked into Joshua's heart for that courage. He also looks into your heart.

What if, in a moment of excitement, Joshua shared with the people God's vision for them, and then a few days later began to waver in his commitment? Commitment climbs when people see consistent passion in the person out front. Commitment is contagious. But if the rigorous demands that accompany the launching of a movement of God discourage this leader early on, he will lose credibility with the people. More importantly, the people will conclude that the vision God revealed was just "another good idea" that has no lasting impact. As a leader:

- You must be able to perceive the new thing God is doing.
- You must be able to see the territory he wants you to conquer.
- You must courageously act upon what God has shown you.

Others will be warmed as they get close to the fire that burns within your heart. Maximum influence begins with the level of your commitment.

Could you picture James Dobson with only a passing interest in matters related to the family? Can you imagine Charles Colson communicating that justice is kind of important and we ought to take a look at our prisons someday? How about Billy Graham only occasionally mentioning that the Bible has some good ideas in it and that people should possibly consider being born again? Think of Bill McCartney suggesting that a man might want to make and keep some promises. Or John Maxwell suggesting ten ways to complete the sentence, "Everything rises and falls with . . ."

No, God has used these men because of their commitment. James Dobson courageously focused on the family. Charles Colson made us squirm as he prophetically highlighted injustice and called for change. Billy Graham passionately preached that the Bible says you must be born again. Bill McCartney filled stadiums by challenging men to permit nothing to stand in the way of their promises. John Maxwell raised up a generation of leaders with the contagious conviction that "Everything rises and falls with leadership." They invested their credibility every day to fulfill their God-given purposes.

Our circle of influence is probably smaller than that of these national leaders, but the courage God requires is the same for all. Joshua had built up a certain amount of credibility with the Israelites. He had previously seen the land they were about to enter. He and Caleb had given a good report after spying out the land and believed they could conquer it even when the majority doubted. He had been an aide to the spiritual giant Moses for as long as anyone could remember. Moses had publicly passed the torch to Joshua: "Now Joshua son of Nun was filled with the spirit of wisdom because Moses had laid his hands on him. So the Israelites listened to him and did what the LORD had commanded Moses" (Deut. 34:9).

Joshua was the chosen successor commissioned by Moses to lead the people where he could not. Now Joshua had to make a choice: Would he selfishly hoard his credibility and simply enjoy the perks of his place of leadership, or would he courageously invest his credibility to see that God's will was done?

Any credibility you have accumulated because of past accomplishments or faithfulness should be courageously offered to God. You must exercise the stewardship of credibility, just as you are to be a good steward of your time, talent, and treasures. To hoard it, or to foolishly spend it, is to squander a God-given resource. You are to invest it so that others might be influenced to obey God.

There is a direct relationship between internal strength and external influence. That's obvious in churches. If a church is spiritually anemic or riddled with internal conflict, its ability to influence the community (or even its youth) is minuscule. If a church is spiritually vibrant and unified, its vision is contagious. The relationship between internal strength and external leadership is seen also in individual leaders. If personal insecurities cause leaders to selfishly pursue their personal agendas, their circle of influence will diminish. If they courageously invest their credibility in the future plans of God, their lives will result in influence with eternal consequence.

I have come to believe that:

- If you have courage, you will influence people based on your convictions.
- If you lack courage, you will influence people based on your comfort zones.
- Courage will take you anywhere you believe God is leading you. Without courage, you will go only where you are comfortable. Will your leadership commitments be based on your convictions or your comfort?

Our staff developed some questions to use as indicators of whether we were choosing comfort over conviction:

- Am I becoming protective of my ministry turf?

One of the primary tasks of spiritual leaders is to raise up new leaders. If I am becoming indispensable or irreplaceable, it's a sign I'm more interested in my future security than in empowering others to be involved in ministry.

- Am I no longer evaluating my ministry effectiveness?

Personal evaluation of one's ministry along with the constructive criticism of others is necessary to refine any endeavor for God. When I start avoiding an honest critique of my programs or accountability for my actions, I'm choosing what's most comfortable.

- Am I emotionally exiting my ministry?

Sometimes difficulties wear us down, and we decide to take a break by convincing ourselves that we just won't care anymore. We go through the motions without the passion because when problems arise, it's more comfortable to be apathetic than emotionally invested in resolving them.

- Am I unwilling to risk failure?

It's most comfortable to only attempt what will be a sure success. However, most people and churches that are trying new things will experience some failures along the way. True change is not a risk-free proposition.

- Am I opting for the familiar over the new?

Am I trying new things, stretching my mind with new thoughts and building my skills by learning new approaches? Growth comes from seeking outside resources and being a continual, lifelong learner. Doing what has always been done is comfortable, yet it erodes the impact of ministry.

- Am I only associating with people whose leadership skills are less developed?

One of the ways we grow is by learning from people who are where we need to be in the future—they are at the point where we would like to be someday. I'm choosing the comfortable when I only choose to be with people who learn from me.

- Am I hanging on to, rather than giving away, ministry opportunities?

Each year, I should seek to give away to others some of what I am currently doing and pick up some new responsibilities. Our staff had a goal to annually give away 20 percent of what we had been doing and replace it with things we needed to do for the future. It's more comfortable to hang on to current responsibilities because we've already developed those skills.

- Am I fulfilling the role the church needs or simply the role I like?

Leaders recognize there are various roles that must be filled in order for an organization to remain healthy and not develop blind spots. A leader must ensure that those roles are in place.

Let me illustrate. At one point, our church board positions were filled by people who tended to be conservative financially. They regularly reviewed cash flow scenarios and budget projections, and any new ministry or building initiatives were carefully tested against our financial capacity. I filled the role of cheerleader—trying to increase their comfort with risk and helping them to take bold steps. As time passed, the membership of our board changed. Most members were no longer fiscally conservative, and at times even seemed disinterested in financial matters. They were ready to go for it, trusting that the finances would be there. My role had to change from cheerleader to red-flag raiser, pointing to the financial ramifications of decisions we were making. Which role would I rather play? Cheerleader. Which role needed to be played? That changed with the constituency of the board. A leader seeks to determine what role is needed, and either fills that role personally or encourages another to fill it. Courage chooses the role that is needed, not the one that is personally preferred.

- Is false humility masking my insecurity?

It can appear like humility not to accept certain leadership positions or not to be involved in particular initiatives. We must always test our hearts to see if this is true humility or simply a cover-up for not doing something that is outside our comfort zone.

All of us occasionally answer these questions positively. We all retreat to our comfort zones when we feel threatened or overwhelmed. But when saying yes to these questions becomes the pattern of our leadership, it's time for a gut check.

Over the years, our church experienced some significant growth. By our sixteenth anniversary, we'd begun our sixth building program. I've discovered that a growing church always requires more money. There's an ongoing need for additional staff and programs. The pastor of a growing church is continually raising money for something.

Asking for money is one of those areas with a high cringe factor. Like fingernails on a blackboard, the discussion of financial need is not music to most people's ears. The higher the cringe factor, the more of the leader's credibility is invested. One of the ways to regularly reinvest whatever credibility you have accumulated is by financially challenging your congregation.

As a matter of conviction, I have no problem with issuing a financial challenge. I believe God wants his people to invest in his work. I believe that giving on earth results in treasures in heaven. I believe spiritual vitality is linked to generosity—that people's hearts are found in what they treasure. But as a matter of comfort, it's another story. The myth that "what a person gives is between him and God" is widely held in our community. I do not relish the opportunity of infringing on what another person considers to be a private matter.

So, I must regularly make a choice. Will I base my leadership on my comfort zones and cause our church to fall short of the necessary funds and our members to be deprived of a meaningful challenge to good stewardship, or will I base my leadership on conviction, transcending my comfort zones to do what is right and empowering people to be part of a movement of God? Comfort or conviction? I regularly face that choice and so do you. It's a matter of courage.

COURAGE FOR OBEDIENCE

Once again, in Joshua 1:7–8, God challenged Joshua to "be strong and very courageous" (1:7). This time, however, it was not the courage to influence others but the courage to carefully obey God's Word. Meditating on it and doing everything in it are the pathways to true success and prosperity. A spiritual leader must be capable of receiving truth from God. Comprehending biblical truth and living it out increases spiritual authority, which is the basis of spiritual leadership.

Stephen Covey, author of the widely read book *The 7 Habits of Highly Effective People*, is convinced that the ability to go through the change process or to make the necessary changes comes from having a "changeless core." That core is nurtured through values and principles that remain consistent even when the winds of change are blowing.[1]

For the Christian leader, those values and principles are revealed in God's Word. The Bible's lasting truths become embedded in our hearts through meditation—"meditate on it day and night" (1:8). There is no substitute for the reading and memorization of the Bible.

My personal accountability goals include a commitment to read through the Bible each year. I must admit that sometimes the daily readings don't seem to be even remotely relevant to my world. I've skipped a few sections of the genealogies and a few of God's pronouncements against nations that no longer exist. But I try to read most of it, and along the way, I am challenged by truths I otherwise might have missed. For instance, while writing these words, I'm wading through the prophecies of Isaiah. As I've recorded my impressions in my journal, I've observed:

- It's dangerous to substitute dependence upon any human alliance for dependence upon God.
- Becoming proud and taking credit for victories that were brought about by the sovereign will of God is a sure way to encounter God's wrath.

Now, alliances with Egypt or the punishment of Assyria may not be today's news, but the principles evident in them are worth meditating upon and incorporating into the changeless core of my life.

Christian leaders also integrate truth into their life through the application of God's Word—"be careful to *do* everything written in it" (1:8, emphasis added). The Bible determines how we act and react in the variety of life situations. A full life is lived from the inside out, and success comes as we obediently pursue God's best:

- If you want a better marriage, learn to love unselfishly and responsively (Eph. 5:22–33).
- If you want a better relationship with your children, devote yourself to learning godly ways of instructing them without exasperating them (Eph. 6:4).
- If you want more freedom or a promotion at work, serve wholeheartedly and work consistently no matter who is present or absent (Eph. 6:5–8).

How you act toward your spouse is not based on how he or she acts toward you. Your treatment of your children is not determined by their treatment of you. Your day's work is not regulated by how the boss treats you or what other employees are doing. You must be careful to do what is written in God's Word. Consistent meditation and application bring about internal transformation. Living inside out means allowing God to change you, not excusing your behavior until God changes someone else.

"Be careful to obey . . . do not turn from it to the right or to the left" (Josh. 1:7). This is one of many commands in Scripture that call for focused obedience:

- "Do not turn aside from any of the commands I give you today, to the right or to the left, following other gods and serving them" (Deut. 28:14).
- "He did what was right in the eyes of the LORD and walked in all the ways of his father David, not turning aside to the right or the left" (2 Kings 22:2).
- "Let us hold unswervingly to the hope we profess, for he who promised is faithful" (Heb. 10:23).

What are the keys to that kind of obedience, that unswerving commitment to a life of integrity before God?

Like most people, I am alarmed by the number of pastors who fail morally. Not only does this devastate their relationship with God, but it has a disillusioning effect on the lives of so many others. Studies have shown that moral failure takes place when two things are true. The first is a neglect of quiet times in God's Word and prayer. The second is the lack of close relationships and accountability. It's hard to stay the course when flying solo. But consistent prayerful meditation on the Word of God and close relationships that provide accountability help reinforce unswerving obedience.

Like Joshua, God wants us to be courageously committed to whole-hearted obedience. The internal victories of obedience to God will develop the character necessary for the external victories that are yet to come.

COURAGE FOR PERSEVERANCE

"Be strong and courageous. Do not be terrified; do not be discouraged" (Josh. 1:9). This is a call for courage that pursues the purposes of God over the long haul. This perseverance can be undermined by two powerful emotions: fear and discouragement.

What are some of the most common fears faced by spiritual leaders?

FEAR OF FAILURE

This one especially haunts those with perfectionist tendencies. In our church leadership team, we made it clear that we expected failure once in a while. If everything we tried must be a guaranteed success, the likelihood of a cutting-edge ministry was remote.

Over the years, we created quite a list of things we would never try again. I discovered, however, that while these attempts may not have turned out as we had envisioned, they often ultimately led to some of the best ministries we ever developed. It takes courage to try it, watch it fall, assess the reasons for its failure, have a good laugh about it, and learn what you need to know so you can try again.

FEAR OF THE UNKNOWN

"We've never done it that way before" can be a symptomatic reaction based on this fear. Just as the familiar is more comfortable, it is also less intimidating.

When we began our Saturday evening worship service in 1992, I remember the apprehension I felt about whether it would be a success. Our conservative community with a heavily Reformed influence was known for its commitment to Sunday as a day of worship. But our three worship services on Sunday morning were not accommodating all who wanted to worship with us, and did not allow us the necessary freedom to develop a significantly different approach to worship. So, we ventured into the unknown, and God blessed our Saturday evening service.

FEAR OF A NEW LEVEL OF COMMITMENT

Leadership in a movement of God committed to taking new territory will inevitably involve steps of personal growth. It's hard to make the necessary changes that allow us to be continually available for what God wants to do in the future.

I've discovered that every time God wants to do something new through me, he also does something new in me. The changes required within can be even more harrowing than the changes required in the surrounding circumstances.

It took courage for Joshua to fight the battles that were ahead and the battles that were within. God reassured Joshua that he need not be terrified because he would be with him (and you) every step of the way.

"Do not be discouraged" (1:9). Discouragement seems to come in two forms:

Dis-courage. This is to be drained of courage. It's when circumstances of life or the criticism of people leaves us empty. It's variously referred to as burn-out or dryness of soul. We're unable to muster the internal fortitude necessary to take the next steps.

Dys-courage. This is dysfunctional courage. It is when we create cheap substitutes for the real thing. It is when we inflate our ego or become insensitive in order to rise above the circumstances of life or the criticism of people. It is the beginning of pride that eventually invites confrontation from our God who "opposes the proud" (James 4:6).

It is a blessing to witness a spiritual leader with a full heart, great courage, and a small ego. Humility is not the opposite of courage; it is a prerequisite for it.

It will take great courage to persevere in the plan God has for you. It is a myth that if God is in it, things will happen easily, naturally, and quickly. In reality, even people and churches who are pursuing God's will have problems that require tremendous courage to endure. We cannot choose whether or not we'll have problems. We can only choose whether the problems we encounter will be those that accompany obedience or disobedience.

We need a theology of suffering to accompany our vision for leadership. Many people falsely assume, "If I'm doing God's will, I'll have health and wealth." The question that people with courage ask is, "If I'm doing God's will and experience pain and poverty, would I still do God's will?" That's the bridge Jesus crossed in the garden of Gethsemane. That's the commitment Paul made as he sat in prison. That's the attitude John exhibited while exiled on the island of Patmos. That's courage.

In their book *You Don't Have to Quit*, Ray and Anne Ortlund detail the lives of biblical characters who encounter three zones.

The A Zone. This marks the initial days of service to God and is characterized by the desire to achieve. It's the honeymoon—everything is new and expectations are high.

The B Zone. This time period is marked by the desire to quit. Initial expectations have proven idealistic. Reality begins to set in and problems begin to emerge. There is an almost irresistible urge to exit the situation or relationship.

The C Zone. This last period is experienced after moving through the B zone, and is characterized by the desire to grow and continue on. It is the most mature of the three zones.[2]

The applications are obvious. We see these zones in marriage relationships, careers, and church leadership. There are scores of people who love obeying God in the A zone but who quickly exit when the B zone is entered. It takes courage to persevere through the fear and discouragement present in the B zone and to finally come to the place of greatest effectiveness in service to God—the C zone.

I remember early in my ministry being puzzled by the frequency with which pastors left their churches immediately after a building program. I now understand that while those who watch from a distance may view a new building as simply exciting, those who provide leadership in making it happen encounter conflicting expectations, financial pressures, long hours, and tough decisions. What looks exciting on the surface can be exhausting behind the scenes. It takes courage to persevere.

One of the greatest gifts we can give each other is encouragement. Like Barnabas in the New Testament, it would be an honor to have the reputation of being an encourager. That comes as we believe the best about others and generously express our support of them as they develop their relationship with God.

But the greatest encouragement can never come to us from another person. It arises out of our relationship with God. Others can't make up the deficit if we fail to experience the courage he wants to build into our lives through our quiet times with him and his presence with us. I remember a seminar speaker who observed, "Most pastors have been taught to be caring, but they've never been taught to be courageous." I can think of no greater teacher than the Holy Spirit—"the Spirit of truth . . . [who] will guide you into all truth" (John 16:13). "Be strong and courageous" (Josh. 1:6).

4

MOVING FORWARD
TOGETHER

Joshua 1:10-18

Momentum Builder	**Momentum Buster**
Momentum is developed when we create an agenda agreement among the team.	Momentum is drained by going it alone.

When I was growing up, the neighborhood kids used to gather in a field behind our house to play baseball. It always started with the two best players choosing sides. The process seemed to take forever, especially for those who were chosen last. One player would make his selection, then the other his selection. Back and forth it went until all were chosen and the teams were formed.

I was usually chosen toward the last, if not the very last. That bothered me. What annoyed me even more was that one of the kids was chosen

> "Vision helps leaders get people very different from the leader and one another to pull together for a common purpose. Failure to build shared vision is the biggest mistake that gifted leaders can make."
>
> —BILL EASUM

before me even though I was the better player. There was a good reason for that—his parents owned a pool. The team he played on got to go swimming after the game. I learned that selections weren't always based on performance; sometimes there were politics involved. He who has the pool makes the team.

> "In all my prayers for all of you, I always pray with joy because of your partnership in the gospel from the first day until now."
>
> —PHILIPPIANS 1:4-5

Even though I know that outside factors sometimes affect who makes the team, I remain convinced that the greatest accomplishments for the kingdom of God will be team efforts. Dreams of divine origin are rarely achieved by going it alone. While individual efforts in many sports may be admirable, God has placed us together in the body of Christ. We need each other. We cannot function without each other (1 Cor. 12:12–27).

Joshua had come to understand that the old chapter of Israel's history was closing and God had chosen to do a new work through him. He had glimpsed at the vision of the Promised Land that God was determined to give his people. He had been challenged by God himself to "be strong and courageous" (Josh. 1:6). Now it was time to go public, to develop a team of people who would initiate God's plan for his people.

I can relate to Joshua. In 1979, Dick Wynn and I saw the vision God laid on our hearts for a new church in the Kentwood community. After personally committing ourselves to this vision, we began to identify others who might launch this new church with us. One day, we sat in his office, a legal pad on the desk and pens in hand, brainstorming the names of those we wanted to personally approach with this vision. There were no programs and no building. We had never met for worship. There were no guarantees. We would need people who believed in God, believed in our leadership, and were willing to take a risk. We needed a team.

Joshua had an advantage. He had officers he could order to get the people moving (1:10). However, a closer look reveals he understood the crucial dimensions of team recruitment. He also understood how indispensable the issue of promise was to the team that would initiate this new movement of God.

A TEAM THAT SHARES IN GOD'S PROMISES

God reveals his promises and his plans in different ways. For some, there is a sense of hearing from God—not an audible voice, but an internal conviction about where God is leading. This is how Joshua received his direction from God, just as Moses had before him.

At other times, God reveals his plans through another person. Perhaps this is how most people become part of a movement of God. A leader like Joshua senses a direction from God and shares that direction with others. Those he shares with must determine if they believe the vision he senses is from God and whether they are convinced they should be part of it. What is the process by which a leader shares his vision and people determine their response to it?

WAITING

Joshua ordered the officers to go through the camp to tell the people that "three days from now" they would cross the Jordan River and enter the land God had promised (1:10–11). Why three days? Maybe that was the time required for them to pack up. Perhaps it allowed time for the spies Joshua sent out to complete their mission (Josh. 2:22). Or maybe it corresponded to the three days Jesus spent in the tomb between his crucifixion and his resurrection.

I believe there is another reason: It was a waiting period. Their leader had told them what he believed God was leading them to do. Now, it was time for the reality of what was ahead to sink in. It was a time for them to decide whether they would own the vision and be part of it. It was a time to weigh the cost and test their willingness to pay the price to have God's very best—the Promised Land.

I remember when we first approached the people we would ask to become leaders in this new church. We organized our presentation to them and visited their homes. We shared with enthusiasm how God had led us to this point. In my youthful zeal, I wanted to close the sale right on the spot—strike while the iron was hot. Dick Wynn made it clear we would lay out the vision and then leave, asking them to prayerfully consider their involvement. We would get back to them in a few days to hear their response. Dick was wisely seeking lasting commitments, not based on an enthusiastic presentation, but on an internal conviction that could only grow in their hearts through prayer—the same way it had grown in our hearts.

Joshua confidently announced where God was leading. I'm sure there were people who wondered if he'd really heard from God or had eaten some day-old manna that caused him to have unusual dreams. Maybe there were some people who left camp, packing up and exiting so they wouldn't have to cross the Jordan River. The majority concluded that this was a mission from God and they wanted to be part of it. It was not just a promise to Joshua, but a promise to them. They came to share in God's promise: "of the land the LORD *your* God is giving *you* for *your* very own" (Josh. 1:11, emphasis added).

In 1995, Kentwood Community Church went through a waiting period that tested the depth of commitment to the vision we believed God had given us. When we received the bids for the construction of our new sanctuary, we were shocked. They came in 50 percent higher than the original estimates. The next Sunday, we announced to the congregation the news we'd received. We could feel the reality set in. We invited people to join us in prayer and wait upon the Lord. We were convinced we had designed the building that was right for our future ministry and were equally convinced we shouldn't borrow more money to meet the additional costs.

As we worked through this waiting period, we came to value the statement, "Where God has put a comma, we dare not put a period," which hung on banners in our current worship center. God used that time to lead us to a new plan of action and a very generous financial response from our congregation. More importantly, he used that time to develop our dependence upon him.

Did everyone stay with us during this time and agree with the direction we sensed God was leading us? No. Some concluded they could not support the direction the congregation was going and chose to leave. It wasn't because they weren't spiritual—in fact, most of them were mature Christians who had hearts for God. It was because they had determined that our church's future direction was not where God was leading them personally, so they chose to attend other churches. That was a bit painful for us. But, for most, God deepened their conviction that the direction we had chosen was his plan and strengthened their commitment to make that vision become a reality. It took a waiting period to accomplish it.

When you share your vision with people, give them time to adjust. This isn't lost time. It may be the most valuable investment of time you ever make. Like waiting on a launch pad while the countdown is underway, it's preparation for expending the energy necessary to get a new initiative off the ground. Waiting is hard, but believing while waiting is harder still—and often necessary for God to do his work.

COMMUNICATING

Joshua also ordered his officers to communicate God's promises to the people: "Go through the camp and *tell* the people" (1:11, emphasis added) what they needed to do in order to prepare to receive God's Promised Land. This communication process was probably the most efficient way to spread the word about what was happening. It served as well to broaden the leadership base beyond Joshua. Perhaps most importantly, every time the leaders (officers) communicated what God was going to do, they came to own it and understand it a little more.

We learn as we listen. But we also learn by passing to others what we have heard or read. Every time someone asks a question, a careful answer clarifies the situation, not only to the one asking the question, but also to the one giving the answer. It is a wise leader who invites others to be part of the communication process. The apostle Paul demonstrated this wisdom when he wrote to Timothy, "And the things you have heard me say in the presence of many witnesses entrust to reliable men who will also be qualified to teach others" (2 Tim. 2:2). Notice the movement of communication:

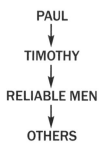

PAUL

↓

TIMOTHY

↓

RELIABLE MEN

↓

OTHERS

It is the means by which God spreads his truth and his vision.

At our church, the board members took part in teaching the membership class. It not only benefited our new members but was a healthy refresher for our board. When our telecare lay ministers made calls to our congregation and community, they were sometimes asked questions they are unable to answer. They found out the answer and responded to the person, so then two people had more fully learned about the church—the caller and the asker. In our congregational chats about ministry initiatives or building expansions, lay leaders as well as pastors made presentations and responded to the issues raised. Both leaders and attendees more clearly grasped what was coming next.

Joshua's leaders shared in God's promises as they communicated them to others. Maybe that's why the Bible identifies one of the qualifications of a leader as the ability to teach (1 Tim. 3:2). Teaching is not the ability to stand in front of a class and lecture but the ability to pass God's Word and work on to others.

PARTICIPATING

Joshua ordered the leaders to spread the word. The people were given the task of getting the supplies ready so they could move out.

Everyone had a part; everyone was participating in some way; everyone was making a contribution to this new movement of God. People worked through change, and Joshua was giving them something to work on. The successful completion of numerous small tasks would culminate in being poised to share in God's promise.

Joshua was an excellent delegator, which was important for two reasons. First, it kept him from spreading himself too thin and becoming too scattered. Second, it gave the people he was leading a sense of involvement in what God was doing. Good delegation lets people feel a little more in control of circumstances and events. It builds their sense of belonging and participation, as well as their commitment to carrying out the change.

Could you imagine Joshua trying to pack up the camp himself? He would have worked himself to the point of exhaustion while people stood around doing nothing. The more time that passed with people standing idly by, the greater the likelihood that complaining would begin.

Maybe Joshua learned the importance of delegation from his mentor, Moses. Moses was a do-it-yourselfer until he was confronted one day by his father-in-law, Jethro.

> When his father-in-law saw all that Moses was doing for the people, he said, "What is this you are doing for the people? Why do you alone sit as judge, while all these people stand around you from morning till evening?" Moses answered him, "Because the people come to me to seek God's will. Whenever they have a dispute, it is brought to me, and I decide between the parties and inform them of God's decrees and laws." Moses' father-in-law replied, "What you are doing is not good. You and these people who come to you will only wear yourselves out. The work is too heavy for you; you cannot handle it alone." (Ex. 18:14–18)

Moses was worn out, and the people were equally exhausted and frustrated because Moses could only be in one place at one time.

This is the way many churches operate. The pastor does it all while the people watch on the sidelines, only to complain when the pastor is not readily available. Or a few lay leaders are exhausted because they tackle every task, great or small. This sets an atmosphere that is conducive to burnout for the few and frustration for the rest.

Creating an environment of shared ownership of the vision and shared leadership in the task involves giving people the opportunity to contribute. Not everyone will be an officer who spreads the word. Some are gifted to be helpers in getting the supplies ready. Getting a job done carries a sense of reward. Achieving a task, especially a tough one, warms the heart and feeds the spirit. It also breeds commitment.

Years ago, a formula that describes the change process was developed. It says that **d**issatisfaction with the way things are, a **v**ision for how they could be, and some **f**irst **s**teps to make that vision a reality must be greater than the natural **r**esistance people have to change: $(D + V + FS) > R$.

If any of those three (dissatisfaction, vision, or first steps) are missing, people will resist the change.

Is this formula as old as Joshua?

Dissatisfaction. Forty years of desert wandering was followed by the death of Moses.

Vision. "I will give you every place where you set your foot" (Josh. 1:3).

First Steps. "Get your supplies ready" (1:11).

Joshua helped them overcome the resistance to change and become part of a movement of God by giving them some practical, attainable steps to get them involved in what God was doing. We can learn from him. If we are dissatisfied with the way things are (it's time to close that chapter) and have a vision for how they should be (a clear statement of our preferred future), then we need to provide some ways in which everyone can be involved in the promises of God.

Joshua was careful not to build this movement around himself or the promises he could make. He led people to share in the promises of God— "Go in and take possession of the land the LORD your God is giving you for your own" (1:11). To make it perfectly clear, he repeated it twice in nearly identical words (1:13, 15). He was building a team that shared in God's promises.

A TEAM OF PEOPLE THAT KEEPS ITS PROMISES

Next, Joshua turned his attention to the two-and-a-half tribes that had made a special arrangement with Moses (1:12–16). These tribes wanted to settle east of the Jordan River because they felt the land was suitable for their very large herds and flocks (see Num. 32). Moses felt this would divide the people of Israel and make it impossible for them to conquer the Promised Land. They swore to him that they would leave their families and flocks behind, cross the Jordan River, and help the rest of the tribes claim their inheritance in the Promised Land, and then return home. Moses agreed to this plan.

Now Joshua was reminding them of their promises. I admire them because they could have offered some excuses that are pretty common in today's society:

1. Too much time has passed—things have changed. In the time since they made their promise to Moses, their herds and families would have grown, so their responsibilities would have changed. Even Moses, the one to whom they had made the promise, was now dead.
2. They already had what they wanted. They had their "promised land," suitable for their purposes. They were not to receive one acre of the land they fought for on the other side of the Jordan River.
3. There would be too many sacrifices. They would miss time with their families. Their flocks and herds would be neglected. They would be risking their lives in battle.

Have you heard those excuses? People who bow out of their marriages because "we were just kids, and so much has changed." People who change their commitment once they have what they want. Or people who change their minds the first time they encounter sacrifice.

God builds his movement through people who keep their promises. I don't think it's a coincidence that one of the greatest spiritual movements of the 1990s was called Promise Keepers. It was (and still is) a movement which calls men to stand by the commitments they have made to God. If Joshua shared the vision with people, he wanted to know they were people he could count on. He wanted to fight the coming battles side-by-side with people who kept their word, not those who would exit at the first sign of difficulty.

One note of caution: We've all been disappointed by people who did not keep their word. It can be disillusioning to discover the person you thought was a spiritual giant is nothing more than a hypocrite. But don't let your disappointment with one person taint your perspective of all people. Godly movements are built on trust, and trust involves the risk that someone will disappoint you. Many have concluded that they will never trust again and so hide their hearts (and their vision) behind walls they build to protect themselves.

Joshua experienced his share of disappointments. After his participation in the spy mission commissioned by Moses, people he had trusted to give a good report gave a bad one (Num. 13:32). He knew what it was like to have people reject his perspective (Num. 14:6–10) and end up representing a minority position in a decision that would dramatically affect his future. Yet he continued to seek out people who kept their promises.

It's worth noting that both Joshua and Moses realized it would take every fighting man of Israel to claim the land that God was about to give them. Their vision was big enough that nine-and-a-half tribes couldn't do what it would take. A God-given vision requires the whole team. Everyone in the body of Christ must function. I regularly told our congregation that we had a vision from God which did not afford the luxury of spectators. We needed everyone's prayers, everyone's spiritual gifts, and everyone's financial stewardship. I also told them that if there ever came a day when our vision had shrunk to the point we didn't need them, I'd apologize—and then I'd pray until God enlarged the vision to the point that we couldn't do it without them once again.

A TEAM THAT MAKES STRONG PROMISES

The final two verses of the first chapter of Joshua record a declaration of allegiance. The men of Israel promised to follow Joshua until the victory was completely won. The penalty for failing to keep that promise was death.

Imagine attending a wedding, expecting the bride and groom to exchange the traditional vows—"for better, for worse, for richer, for poorer, in sickness and in health, until death do us part." Instead, they promise to stay together "for better, for worse, for richer, for poorer, in sickness and in health—and if I don't, you can kill me." Or imagine signing a contract for a loan. The penalty for falling behind in payments is not additional interest, but the threat of death.

I'm not suggesting that the Israelites' pledge of "obedience unto death" should provide a pattern for all promises. It did, however, strongly express their commitment to doing whatever it took to lay hold of the future vision God had given them. It also gave evidence of their willingness to submit to Joshua's authority and follow his leadership.

J. Robert Clinton, in his book *The Making of a Leader*, asserts that "leaders who have trouble submitting to authority will usually have trouble exercising spiritual authority."[1] Many people are attracted to leadership because of the power and prestige they believe it will provide. This attraction is often based in a proud spirit, which the Bible consistently declares invites the opposition of God: "God opposes the proud, but gives grace to the humble" (James 4:6). Spiritual authority is not humanly generated by a grasp for power but is obtained through a willingness to be a servant of all—beginning with submission to God. Spiritual authority is built on a foundation of humility and a willingness to follow when God's plan calls for strong followers.

Their pledge of allegiance included more than a commitment to follow. It contained words of encouragement. The phrase "be strong and coura-geous" was first given to Joshua by his mentor Moses (Deut. 31:6–7, 23). Then they were communicated directly from God to Joshua (Josh. 1:6–7, 9). Now, they were coming from those Joshua would lead.

EXPECT A VARIETY OF RESPONSES WHEN RECRUITING A TEAM

Sometimes leaders are surprised by the wide variety of reactions people have to their vision. Some naïvely assume that if a vision is from God, all the people who hear its presentation will respond positively. As I've shared our vision for ministry over the years, I've noticed five different types of responses.

REFRESHERS

These are people who inspire you to dream great dreams and attempt great things for God. They may encourage you through personal affirmation. Their investments in your life may enable you to reach higher than you would otherwise. I've noticed that some of the refreshers in my life don't even know me personally. By reading their books, hearing them speak, or watching them in action, I'm inspired.

REFINERS

Refiners sharpen your ideas and clarify your vision. This might be accomplished through constructive criticism or through their ability to ask provocative questions. It happens through people who eagerly want to receive your vision but can't quite seem to grasp it. As you struggle to make it clear to them, it becomes clearer to you.

REFLECTORS

Some people simply reflect your vision and energy. They don't create any energy themselves, nor do they detract from the momentum of your vision. They are usually agreeable, pleasant people to have around—they are faithful people.

REDUCERS

These folks seek to reduce your vision to their comfort zones. They resist the areas of your vision that represent what they consider to be undesirable changes. They may agree with the risk-free dimensions of your plan but resist those which make them uncomfortable.

REJECTERS

Rejecters will never adopt your vision. They will either exit or stay and drag their feet in an attempt to frustrate you until you exit. They drain momentum and enthusiasm.

As I've encountered these various responses, I've drawn the following conclusions that help me in relating to them.

First, I used to assume that I really needed the first two groups, I would enjoy the middle group, and I should watch out for the last two groups. I now believe that all responses are helpful in clarifying and communicating a vision.

Second, the first two groups are usually busy and productive people. If you want their input, you have to seek them out rather than wait for them to come to you. If you only respond to those who come to you, the feedback you receive may be skewed. Often it's those who feel most negative that are strongly motivated to make their feelings known. This is why many pastors spend almost all their time with negative people, and many church boards have agendas that are nothing more than responding to problems. I deliberately initiate appointments with people I believe will refresh and refine our church's vision.

Third, when you're drained of energy, it's easiest to spend your time with the reflectors. These are nice people who are faithful, supportive, and pleasant to be around. It's obvious that there might be a tendency to avoid the last two groups—the reduction or rejection of your vision causes a drain of energy. But there is also a tendency to avoid the people who stretch you or ask the probing questions, which, if continued over a period of time, is a prescription for mediocrity.

Last, remember that the initial response to any substantive change is resistance. Another benefit of sharing your vision and allowing time for people to process it (the waiting period mentioned earlier) is that it permits them to work through the natural resistance that first arises. Don't label people as rejecters or reducers when they may, after working through a brief period of resistance, be your strongest supporters.

Expect a variety of responses. Just because you believe you have received a vision from God, don't assume people will receive it from you without a variety of responses. It takes wisdom to capitalize on each of these responses in order to make your vision a reality.

Recruiting a team is hard work, yet it is some of the most necessary work for the leader. The potential within a church is directly related to its leadership team. In growing as a leader, be sure your team grows with you. If you're expanding as a church, monitor whether or not a corresponding expansion is taking place in the leadership base. Constantly equipping, enlarging, and upgrading a team of leaders is an indispensable dimension of a movement of God.

5

TIME FOR A
REALITY CHECK

Joshua 2

Momentum Builder	**Momentum Buster**
Momentum is developed by setting realistic goals and action plans.	Momentum is drained by failing to survey obstacles and opportunities.

"Rejoice with those who rejoice; mourn with those who mourn" (Rom. 12:15). Serving as a pastor provides plenty of opportunities for both rejoicing and mourning. On more than one occasion, I've left a joyful wedding celebration to officiate at a funeral. In one appointment, I listened to a person share the joy of a dream come true. In the next, I empathized with a person whose dream was irreparably broken. Ministry is a mixed bag of experiences.

From time to time, people share with me their dreams of starting a new business. They talk about the freedom it will give them to be their

> "Realistic leaders are objective enough to minimize illusions. They understand that self-deception can cost them their vision."
> —BILL EASUM

own boss, the money they will make, and the influence they will have on others. These stories intrigue me because of my early desires to enter the business world. I delight in their dreams but also sense another responsibility—to match them with others who have walked that road.

> "Now listen, you who say, 'Today or tomorrow we will go to this or that city, spend a year there, carry on business and make money.' . . . Instead, you ought to say, 'If it is the Lord's will, we will live and do this or that.'"
> —JAMES 4:13, 15

There are some harsh realities that commonly accompany the initiation of a new business. Those who envision being their own boss soon discover they will have many bosses called customers. Their business plans map a road to profitability in one year, when in reality, it may require a decade to turn the first real profit. Others who have been there and done that can provide a reality check for them. These glimpses of reality should not limit or determine the vision but can enlighten the potential business owner as to what it will take to accomplish the vision.

Likewise, spiritual leaders must make a realistic assessment of the obstacles and opportunities involved in a new step of faith. Sometimes this can be done by the leaders alone, but most times it is beneficial to garner the input of others. This reality check allows for the creation of relevant action plans to carry out a God-given vision.

Joshua 2 records a spy mission organized by Joshua as the Israelites prepared to enter the Promised Land. He formed a task force of two and gave a clear mandate of what they were to accomplish. From Joshua and his spies, we learn the bases that need to be covered as we scout out new territory to be taken for God.

CHECK WHAT YOU'VE LEARNED FROM PAST EXPERIENCE

This was not the first time spies were sent to scout the Promised Land. The last spy mission had been initiated by Moses, and Joshua had been one of those spies (see Num. 13–14). I believe Joshua 2:1 reflects some changes Joshua made as a result of past experience.

JOSHUA SECRETLY RECRUITED THE SPIES

When Moses had sent out the spies, they were selected publicly and were allowed to give a public report (Num. 13:26–33). This resulted in a disaster that cost a movement of God forty years of potential progress, perhaps because they reported to people who didn't have the faith or the vision to process the realities without being unduly frightened by them (Num. 14:1–4); or perhaps in that public setting, the spies veered from their original mandate. Their commission was to provide information about the Promised Land (Num. 13:17–20, 27–29), not their opinion about whether it could be done (13:31–33). Their official, public report (13:26) degenerated into a subversive, negative report (13:32). The ten rebellious spies, capitalizing on their visibility and experience, spread among the Israelites a bad report.

Joshua sent the spies out secretly. They were not commissioned publicly, nor were they ever given the opportunity to report publicly. They formed a task force that was to provide him with information about the obstacles and opportunities of the Promised Land. He wanted to see how much things had changed in the forty years since he had scouted the territory himself.

Observations for Today's Leaders. When forming a task force to investigate a new step of faith, determine if their report is to only include information or if they are to give an evaluation of the feasibility of this new step. It should be made clear how and to whom they are to report. Is their work to be somewhat confidential until those who have decision-making authority have had an opportunity to review and respond to their conclusions? It can be very beneficial when recruiting task force members to have a healthy up-front conversation about the report being given to the appropriate people. Underscore the negative impact of spreading the report to people who may not be ready to face the challenges until the leaders can give direction.

JOSHUA SENT TWO SPIES

Moses had sent out twelve spies, one to represent each of the twelve tribes (Num. 13:2–16). Their participation in the spy mission was based on their position in the tribal structure of the nation of Israel. It seemed to be a good idea to have a delegation representative of the people of God. Later, however, it becomes evident that only two of them (Joshua and Caleb) had the faith required to participate in such a mission. This resulted in changing God's guarantee of victory (13:2) into a maybe.

Joshua sent out two spies. He was making the transition from leadership based on position (representatives from each tribe) to leadership based on conviction (a firm belief in God's promises). A glimpse of their faith is found in their later conversation with Rahab. They promised to treat her kindly if she upholds her end of the bargain, not if the Lord gives them the land, but when the Lord gives them the land (Josh. 2:14).

Observations for Today's Leaders. Many times boards and committees are formed based on representation of various groups within the church. While this is great if there are enough people of faith to represent the various groups, this commitment can be disastrous if negative people are chosen just because of their position in a certain group. Many church boards, in an effort to have broader representation, have expanded in a way that results in diluted faith and needless wandering.

JOSHUA FOCUSED THEIR EFFORTS ON JERICHO

When Moses sent out the twelve spies, he gave them a broad assignment: to explore the land (Num. 13:16–20). The assignment may have been too broad, resulting in a mission that took forty days to accomplish. They were gone so long that they began to magnify the barriers and minimize the blessings (13:27–29). They began to weigh only the cost of doing something—of moving forward with God's plan—and lost sight of the cost of doing nothing—of standing still in disobedience to God's plan.

Police departments often use undercover officers to get the information they need. At times, these officers can be out of contact with the department for an extended period of time. If this deep cover operation goes on too long, these officers may forget to whom they are accountable and in which world they really belong. The result can be the loss of officers and a failed mission.

Joshua commissioned his task force to "look over the land," but "especially Jericho" (Josh. 2:1). The focus on Jericho allowed them to complete their work in just a few days and return to their people.

Observations for Today's Leaders. When creating a task force to provide realistic action plans that overcome the obstacles, carefully focus on their responsibilities and establish a realistic time frame. Nearly anyone who spends too much time focusing on financial, facility, or personnel limitations can begin to lose faith. These limitations must be realistically identified yet not allowed to loom too large as a result of continual focus upon them.

Joshua learned from his past experiences. He did not ignore reality by skipping a spy mission completely. Like Jesus, he realized the wisdom of counting the cost (Luke 14:25–35). However, the way he structured the mission reflects the wisdom of experience. Spiritual leaders, when taking a new step of faith, should ask, "Have we tried anything similar in the past, and what did we learn?" That willingness to learn from previous experiences develops wisdom and can prevent catastrophe.

CHECK OUT WHAT OTHERS HAVE TO SAY

The spies embarked on their mission and ended up at the house of Rahab (Josh. 2:1–7). Before the spies went to sleep for the night, Rahab went up on the roof to talk to them (2:8–11). From this conversation, the spies learned some things that must have greatly encouraged their hearts. First, Rahab knew God had given them the land and that those who lived there were melting in fear because of the impending invasion of God's people. Second, the people of the land had heard what God had done to others (the Egyptians and the Amorites) who had tried to stand in the way of his plan. They knew God's track record of victory. Last, their hearts had melted and courage had failed, "for the LORD your God is God in heaven above and on the earth below" (2:11). The power of the God of Israel knows no boundaries. Sometimes the confirmation of a movement of God comes from the most unexpected sources. This pagan woman and her people were probably more convinced of the power of God than the average Israelite.

A reality check involves listening to the viewpoints of others and actively seeking their input. There are different levels of listening. At the most superficial level, listening is focused on words alone. On a deeper level, listening moves beyond what is communicated verbally and an attempt is made to grasp what a person is feeling. This involves not only what is said but the reason why it is said. For the spiritual leader, there is yet a deeper level of listening. Beyond the words and feelings, it is looking for evidence that God is preparing the way for what he wants to do.

To whom should we listen when conducting a reality check? When preparing for a major new initiative, I attempt to gather input from many different groups of people.

PEOPLE WHOSE NEEDS MAY BE MET

Listen to people whose needs will potentially be met. This will help determine if there is a niche for that ministry and what steps should be taken to meet that need. It can be dangerous to assume that we know what people need or to simply duplicate what has been done elsewhere to meet similar needs.

When we began a singles ministry, we assumed singles would want to study issues and challenges relevant to being a single adult. Our assumption was wrong. While our core group wanted to have occasional seminars addressing the single person's needs, they wanted their class curriculum to focus on spiritual and emotional maturity for the Christian adult. Listening to our singles helped us to correct our false assumptions before the ministry started off on the wrong foot.

PEOPLE WITH RESOURCES

Listen to people who have the resources to meet the need. These resources may be financial or spiritual gifts that address the need or experience in that ministry area. Just because a need exists does not mean God is calling a church to meet that need. It's wise to evaluate available resources of people, space, and finances.

Many people over the years offered suggestions regarding programs they wanted us to offer. Often they were sharing something they had witnessed in another church or parachurch organization. We asked if they were willing to help initiate that ministry, and we also sometimes voiced the idea to others who might have the resources to help launch or sustain it. We learned that if no one stepped forward to provide leadership or support, it was best to place the suggestion in a future-idea file until God raised up the required workers.

PEOPLE ON THE OUTSIDE

Listen to people outside the walls of the church. I regularly asked our community leaders what they perceived as needs in our city. I talked to unchurched people about what a church could do to meet a particular need. Sometimes I talked to other church leaders in the community to see what they had tried to do or were currently doing.

At least once a year, I made an appointment with our city's mayor and superintendent of schools. They witnessed changes in our geographical area that helped determine our approach to outreach. This kept us from becoming ingrown by only listening to information from those in our church.

PEOPLE WHO ARE SKEPTICAL

Listen to the skeptics—those who believe something can't or shouldn't be done. They'll point out the pitfalls and prejudices associated with a new territory of ministry. You don't have to agree with them, nor do you need to convince them they are wrong. Learn from them what makes people uncomfortable and where resistance may be encountered.

For years, we conducted multiple worship services on Sunday morning. This trend was picking up momentum as facility costs increased and people's desires for options also increased. When we adjusted service times, we tried to listen to people who didn't like our suggested schedule. We tried to discover why they were skeptical of it. This helped us anticipate problems and, when possible, find solutions.

PEOPLE WITH EXPERIENCE

Listen to people who have already done what you are considering. Learn from their experiences as well as from your own. Gleaning insights from the experiences of others can lead to having much better experiences yourself.

As we began the construction of our new sanctuary, I became concerned about the potential impact of moving into a sanctuary three times the size of our existing one. I conducted interviews with the leaders of others churches who had made similar transitions. I noted their responses to my questions about how the physical move had affected the culture of their churches. Among my discoveries:

- Their congregations struggled with the new building not feeling the same. The congregational singing wasn't as resounding because the new facility was roomier. The fellowship didn't seem as close because members were no longer bumping into one another in crowded hallways or packing the pews as tightly. Some people concluded that because the worship and fellowship didn't seem the same, God wasn't as present in the new facilities as he had been in the old.
- The expectations for every dimension of ministry were higher. The choir should sing better and the pastor should have better sermons in this new and improved sanctuary. This increase in expectations was subtle yet powerful, and led some to be disappointed with the ministry of the church. Like putting a familiar picture in a brand new frame, the ministry didn't look the same anymore.
- Some of the churches experienced a decrease in volunteers. Lay ministers were intimidated and struggled with whether or not they were good enough to serve in the new surroundings. As the facilities influenced expectations, the volunteers' sense of inadequacy was amplified.

These are just a few of the insights I gleaned from their experiences. I relayed these interviews to our leaders, hoping to anticipate the transitions our congregation would face and plan accordingly. It is true that we shape the design of our facilities, and then they shape us.

Choosing a cross section of people who view an initiative from different perspectives can provide a picture of whether God is preparing the way for that endeavor.

The need to be seeker sensitive is widely discussed by churches today. Willow Creek Community Church and Pastor Bill Hybels have led the way, highlighting the needs of "un-churched Harry" to develop a focus for ministry. But Joshua's spies long ago demonstrated seeker sensitivity by listening to the perspectives of "un-churched Rahab." They listened to her fears and hopes. They listened to her view of their God and what they might do to meet her needs. Undoubtedly, what they learned shaped their final report to Joshua.

CHECK TO BE CERTAIN ALL BASES HAVE BEEN COVERED

A reality check that only investigates one aspect of the anticipated initiative isn't a reality check at all. This task force of two spies sought a vision of what was ahead that would cover all the realities. Their vision of the Promised Land was three-dimensional.

A VISION OF CONDEMNATION (JOSH. 2:9–11)

The two spies were given a glimpse of a world condemned by God. They witnessed the fear and despair of people who faced judgment. With Rahab's help, they looked beyond the defenses and defiance to see the lordship of God both in heaven and on earth, even in this pagan land. That was the beginning point of their vision, and should be the beginning point of any vision a church develops.

This vision of condemnation is very different from the common vision of society today. We live in a country that believes people are basically good—in spite of the Bible's clear teaching and the abundant evidence in the daily news. If the church's vision was in contrast to this view of the goodness of man, that would provide some hope. But even the church acts increasingly as if salvation is universal and that everyone will make it somehow. While this may not be publicly stated, many Christians fail to share their faith in their circles of influence, comforting themselves with the thought that their contacts will make it to heaven because they are basically good people.

Do we really believe that people who do not submit their lives to God end up in hell? Do we have a vision of people condemned if they don't take advantage of the opportunity to respond to God in repentance? At Kentwood Community Church, our leaders occasionally took tours of the surrounding community to allow God to break our hearts for people condemned apart from Christ. We drove to the schools and pictured the eternal destiny of young people. We drove through wealthy neighborhoods and reminded ourselves that money cannot provide salvation. We toured neighborhoods where poverty was present and remembered that the greatest poverty is not financial but spiritual. Every decision we make must include the reality of condemned people.

At times, the book of Joshua is criticized because the people who previously inhabited the land were killed. What chances, however, would these people have had for eternal life if the Israelites had never invaded the land? Rahab made it clear they already knew about God and could have chosen to submit to his plans. Every victory in the Promised Land was an opportunity for repentance—an opportunity for condemned people like Rahab to become consecrated people devoted to God and his purposes in the world.

A VISION OF SALVATION (JOSH. 2:12–14)

Lost people matter to God. We must ask the question, "Were the spies only sent to check out the Promised Land in preparation for invasion?" While I'm convinced that was the primary purpose, I'm also convinced God spotted Rahab's faith from a long way off. This mission demonstrates the lengths to which God will go for the salvation of a soul and her family.

Spiritual leaders must remind themselves how much lost people matter to God. From the first verse most people learn (John 3:16) to the three parables Jesus shares in Luke 15 (lost sheep, lost coin, and lost son), the Bible emphasizes that God is in the business of seeking and finding lost people. The scarlet cord Rahab hangs from her window has been a symbol throughout church history of the blood of Christ shed for lost people. The reality of God's heart for the lost compels us to act courageously to reach them.

A VISION OF ACTION (JOSH. 2:17–21)

The spies committed themselves to rescue Rahab and her relatives. Their vision resulted in an action plan. Rahab acted on her faith by covering for the spies, hanging out the scarlet cord, and gathering her relatives into her house. Her example of faith combined with works later led James to include her as an example of faith in action (James 2:25).

While we must sense the brokenness of people in our world and the heart God has for them, we must go beyond mere sentimentalism to develop realistic action plans. We must move beyond how we feel about it to what we will do about it.

This three-dimensional vision is indispensable to any new ministry initiative. Without a vision for condemnation, we will not see the eternal difference our actions can make. Without a vision for salvation, we may judge the lost but not reach them. Without a vision for action, our faith is impotent. Like a three-legged stool, all legs must be present to support the taking of new territory.

CHECK OUT ALL CONDITIONS BEFORE
MAKING YOUR COMMITMENTS

Rahab asked the spies for a commitment (Josh. 2:12–13) to show kindness to her and her family by preserving their lives. The spies indicated their willingness to meet her request, but set certain conditions for their commitment:

- Rahab could not tell anyone what the spies were doing (2:14). She had to keep their mission a secret to prevent the residents of the land from making special preparations for their attack.
- Rahab had to hang a scarlet cord from her window (2:18). The spies might not remember the exact location of her house when they returned and could not be responsible for going house to house to find her when a battle was raging.
- Rahab had to gather into her house the family members she wanted saved from destruction by the Israelites (2:18). Not only would this be a demonstration of some level of faith among the family members, but it would be impossible to attempt to locate all of her relatives during the course of the battle.

While the spies were very grateful for what Rahab had done and greatly encouraged by her report of the preparatory work God had done, their enthusiasm did not result in unrealistic commitments. Their conditions raise questions that wise spiritual leaders ask, such as:

- What happens if another person does not do what he or she promised? If Rahab did not uphold her end of the bargain, the deal was off. As church leaders, we need to ask, "What happens if people do not follow through on the financial pledges they have made? What happens if volunteers for a ministry back out? What happens if the space is no longer available?"
- Are my commitments realistic under the conditions? The spies knew their promises would have to be kept in the midst of a battle. Spiritual leaders assess such conditions as available finances, time, and willing volunteers as they make their commitments.
- Do my commitments obligate others, and am I authorized to speak for them? The spies had been given the right to speak for Joshua and were obligating him by their promise. When a leader makes a commitment for others, he or she must be certain to have the authority to speak for those people.

These are the questions we asked when we were raising money and securing financial arrangements for the new sanctuary. We also asked questions like these when we established a partnership with our denomination for planting new Wesleyan churches in Cambodia. Making realistic commitments requires an assessment of the conditions under which those commitments will be carried out.

CHECK IF YOUR CONCLUSIONS REPRESENT BOTH FACTS AND FAITH

The spies returned to Joshua and gave their report (2:23–24). Their conclusions were an appropriate blend of fact and faith:

- Fact: They "told him everything that had happened to them" (2:23).
- Faith: "The LORD has surely given the whole land into our hands; all the people are melting in fear because of us" (2:24).

When pursuing God's purpose, both facts and faith are necessary. It is a challenge to determine the appropriate blend.

When we made decisions at our church, we always wanted to make wise decisions. Wisdom cannot be developed unless we relate God's perspectives to the realities of life. There is no such thing as blind faith. In fact, what makes Christian faith so unique is its ability to face the realities and yet have hope that transcends those realities. The most powerful example is the ability of Christians to face the awful intrusion of death upon God's design for life, yet through his grace, they realize that death is but sleep before they awaken in God's presence. In the same way, we can realistically face the obstacles of any new initiative and not be limited by them. The process of seeing God at work as we face the challenges develops wisdom.

We also wanted to make faith-stretching decisions. We wanted to take new territory for God and move beyond our comfort zones. This faith did not ignore the reality check but allowed God to lead us as we made our way through it.

6

FOCUSING ON PRIORITIES

Joshua 3:3–4

Momentum Builder	**Momentum Buster**
Momentum is developed by humbly creating a God-focused movement.	Momentum is drained by pridefully establishing a man-centered movement.

During one Saturday night service, Rob shared his life story. Having grown up going to church, he had gone through the motions of making a commitment to Christ at various points in his childhood and teenage years. As the years progressed, he decided to stop pretending and to start "enjoying" life. He spent much of his time partying, his greatest point of pride being the amount of alcohol he could consume. He graduated from alcohol to marijuana, convincing himself that his daily use of it didn't mean he was a pothead. It simply helped his aching body after a day's work on the cement crew.

> "It is extremely easy for us to give our major
> attention to minor things."
> —E. C. McKENZIE

During this time, he met the girl he wanted to marry, and on a special occasion, she wanted to give him a gift. He requested a gold cross to wear around his neck. It wasn't the religious nature of the symbol that made him choose a cross. He just viewed it as a cool piece of jewelry to wear on a daily basis. Little did he know the impact it would have on his life.

> "Since, then, you have been raised with Christ, set your hearts on things above, where Christ is seated at the right hand of God. Set your minds on things above, not on earthly things."
> —COLOSSIANS 3:1–2

When he got ready for work in the morning, the cross was reflected in the mirror. When he prepared for bed at night, he felt the cross around his neck. It seemed to enlarge as time went on. He couldn't help but focus on it, and it became a powerful reminder of all he had learned in his childhood at church. He also became keenly aware of how out of sync his life was with what the cross represented. His growing attention to that cross was used by God to bring conviction to his heart and, finally, commitment of his life to Christ.

What you focus on can influence the direction of your life. Focus can determine the difference between success and failure. I learned that while I was young. My dad would say, "Keep your eye on the ball," as he pitched baseballs to me. My grandpa would say, "Focus on that mark on the lane," as I threw my bowling ball down the alley. My teachers would say, "Keep your eyes on your own paper," as my classmates and I took tests.

Focus is important beyond the world of sports and school. Businesses that lose their strategic focus may see their profit margins disappear. Couples who fail to pay attention to their marriage slowly but surely become strangers. Organizations that lose sight of their mission statements soon wallow in mediocrity. Churches that fail to center on Christ trade a ministry of eternal consequence for activity with temporary impact.

Focusing on God can create great expectations that can lead to great endeavors. As Joshua prepared to move the people into the Promised Land, there was no mystery as to what the focal point was. It was the ark of the covenant. This piece of tabernacle furniture is mentioned nine times in seventeen verses. It symbolizes two important dimensions that are indispensable to all who seek to be part of a movement of God.

A REFERENCE POINT FOR GOD'S PEOPLE

As Joshua and the Israelites stood on the brink of the Jordan River anticipating entry into the Promised Land, the officers went throughout the camp giving orders to the people: "When you see the ark of the covenant of the LORD your God, and the priests, who are Levites, carrying it, you are to move out from your positions and follow it. Then you will know which way to go, since you have never been this way before" (3:3–4). The ark served as a reference point, indicating when they were to move out and which way they were to go.

Notice that the officers did not focus attention on the obstacles. The Jordan River, which flowed between the Israelite camp and the Promised Land, was not a meandering creek. It was at flood stage (3:15), likely flowing rapidly and making any crossing precarious. The people could have easily become discouraged if they focused on the obstacle ahead. While reality checks are important and obstacles need to be noted, they are not the center of attention in any endeavor of faith.

The officers also did not focus on Joshua, other officers, priests, or any other leaders. Man-centered movements achieve temporary success at best. Spiritual leaders demonstrate great wisdom when they fulfill their roles in a movement of God without seeking to become the center of attention. The temptation to take God's place is based on pride and is as old as the rebellion of Satan. It invites God's opposition instead of God's blessing—"God opposes the proud but gives grace to the humble" (James 4:6).

Paradoxically, it was a day when the Lord told Joshua he would be exalted—"Today I will begin to exalt you in the eyes of all Israel, so they may know that I am with you as I was with Moses" (Josh. 3:7). This day was going to build credibility for Joshua—people would begin to compare his leadership to that of his predecessor and mentor, Moses. Joshua was to do his part and let God determine who needed to be exalted to move his plan forward.

While leaders need a certain amount of visibility to fulfill their roles in God's movement, that visibility must always be offered to God for his purposes. No one should be indispensable except the Head of the Church, Jesus Christ. Any human substitute for the headship of Christ will result in a loss of the staying power necessary for lasting fruit in ministry.

For the Israelites, the focus was not on the obstacles or the human leaders. Their reference point was the ark of the covenant. So, should your church go out and purchase an ark? Hardly. What should our reference point be today? A closer look at what the ark of the covenant represented provides the answer.

First, the ark represented the presence of God. It was kept in the Holy of Holies, the most sacred part of the tabernacle where the *shekinah* glory of God resided. Representations of two angelic beings with wings raised stood on its lid. The mercy seat rested beneath the wings (and on top of the ark). God was present and his mercy could be found there.

Second, the ark contained the Word of God. Inside were the tablets of stones on which were recorded the Ten Commandments (Heb. 9:4). These Ten Commandments represented the core values, the nonnegotiable authoritative will of God for his people. The ark contained the written Word of God and symbolized his authority over his people.

Today, by his Spirit, God resides in us. His Spirit guides us through conviction and affirmation, and "testifies with our spirit that we are God's children" (Rom. 8:16). We also have God's written Word, the Bible. We give it a place of authority over our tradition, reason, and experience. God's Word and Spirit provide our reference point. No wonder Jesus tells the woman at the well that "true worshipers will worship the Father in spirit and truth" (John 4:23).

The ark of the covenant helps us not only understand what our reference point should be, but when we should be especially careful to focus on that reference point. While it's true we should always be sensitive to God's Spirit and responsive to his Word, there are some occasions when we must be strategically focused on God. A quick survey of Joshua reveals how the ark was utilized to bring the Israelites' focus back to their Creator.

DURING NEW INITIATIVES

The Israelites were preparing to enter the Promised Land (Josh. 3–4). The territory was unfamiliar to them—"you have never been this way before" (3:4). Because they had never been there or done that, they were to focus on the ark so they would know which way to go. Joshua didn't allow the people to remain where they were and become completely familiar with the new territory before moving them on. There are some things that cannot be known unless one moves ahead. He pointed them to something that was familiar to them (the ark) as they entered a land that was unfamiliar (Canaan).

I've discovered that people don't have to completely grasp the vision or understand the whole action plan to move forward in God's will. Some things cannot be fully comprehended until after they have been acted upon. The key to moving beyond comfort zones is being focused on the leadership of God's Spirit.

The launching of a new ministry initiative is a great time for a prayer meeting. It's an opportune time to review the biblical reasons for what is being done.

DURING TIMES OF CONFLICT

The Israelites followed the ark of the covenant into battle against Jericho (Josh. 6). This is one of many times that Scripture records the ark being carried into a conflict. It was a visible reminder of God's presence in the midst of the conflict and of the victory that God would ultimately provide.

A renewed focus on God's Word and Spirit during times of conflict is vital for spiritual leaders. If there is conflict in a marriage, rather than the individual partners focusing on their needs and desires, they should listen to the inward promptings of the Spirit and see what the Bible says their response should be. If there is emotional turmoil, rather than being overwhelmed by feelings, a person should focus on God and seek the peace that transcends understanding. If spiritual warfare is taking place, remember the heavenly armor (Eph. 6:10–18) designed to equip Christians to overcome the Enemy.

The proper focus is also crucial during times of conflict within the church. So many church fights are really personality clashes over trivial matters. Why do people fight over the color of the carpet or which pew to sit in? Is it because the color scheme or the seating arrangement will influence effectiveness in fulfilling the Great Commission? No, people have failed to set their hearts and minds on things above (Col. 3:1–2) and instead have focused on the trivial.

DURING TIMES OF FAILURE AND CONFUSION

After being defeated in battle by the people of Ai, Joshua and the elders of Israel fell face down before the ark (Josh. 7:6). It should have been an easy victory for them, and they didn't understand why this had happened until God informed them of the sin of Achan.

Failure tends to create a self-centered focus often accompanied by a pity party. "Woe is me" introspection has limited benefit and, at times, may even cause us to miss what God is saying to us in the aftermath of failure. While I wish I could learn all of life's lessons from successful ventures, there are many principles better taught from failure. A soul that is searching for God's leading is a way to capitalize on setbacks.

DURING TIMES OF WORSHIP

After Ai was finally destroyed, Joshua brought the ark into a public covenant renewal service (8:30–35). At their best, worship services are centered on God's Word and led by God's Spirit.

Tragically, most public church services are not God-centered. The majority of people leave, asking, "Did that service meet my needs?" not, "What biblical principles did I discover that I can use to honor God this week?" They exit, wondering, "Did that service fulfill my expectations?" instead of, "Did I worship in a way that was responsive to God's

Spirit?" Increasingly, worship services are man-centered—designed to entertain and satisfy the consumer mentality of attenders.

Those may seem harsh words, and they are certainly not meant to excuse poorly planned services or irrelevant messages. A proper focus on God is easier to attain when the service flows according to a biblical theme. When people have prepared thoroughly, they offer their best to God. But if human preferences are the reference point for worship rather than praise to an awesome God, something is wrong.

So how do churches establish God's Word and Spirit as the reference point of their ministries?

- Be sure that prayer is regularly included in various meetings in the life of the church—not perfunctory prayers, but those which sincerely invite God's will to be done. Don't limit prayer to the beginning or end of those sessions, but pause spontaneously for prayer.

- Build worship services around biblical themes such as praise, repentance, obedience, or sacrifice. Weave scriptural references into the worship service's theme.

- During decisive moments in your church's history, hold special services that devote time to prayer and relevant Bible study. For instance, on our church's sixteenth anniversary, our evening service was a concert of prayer built around the song of Moses recorded in Deuteronomy 32. Moses used a review of history as an occasion for giving God praise, seeking forgiveness, and promising submission to God's will for the future. During our anniversary service, we recounted the history of our church. We offered praise, sought forgiveness, and committed ourselves to a future that honors God.

- Bathe any significant change or ministry initiative in prayer. A consultant employed by churches within our district has wisely counseled that the first item on the agenda of the pastors and lay leaders should be the formation of intercessory prayer groups. He has observed that lasting, spiritually significant changes will not happen unless the Holy Spirit is earnestly sought to create an atmosphere in which they can thrive.

REVERENCE FOR GOD'S POWERFUL PRESENCE

In general, I appreciate the concern for seeker sensitivity in worship. Spiritual leaders recognize the needs of non-religious people and build bridges to carry the gospel to them. Pastors evaluate the style and content of their messages to see if they are connecting with people who are biblically illiterate but genuine seekers. Local churches are more active in influencing their various communities rather than withdrawing from them. The danger, however, is in losing perspective. We must always remember that God is our ultimate audience. Losing sight of that focal point leaves a church with a superficial ministry that only caters to the whimsical desires of fickle people and communicates "what their itching ears want to hear" (2 Tim. 4:3).

Our church wrestles with the constant tension between relevance and reverence. We seek to be relevant to our culture without losing reverence for God. When I was growing up, there were more reminders of the need for reverence. The pastor was referred to as Reverend; today our congregation calls me Wayne, or sometimes Pastor Wayne. The room where we held public services was called a sanctuary; today we call ours an auditorium. The entryway was once called a narthex; now we have a lobby. We're pretty casual and informal, and that's more comfortable for people who aren't used to being in church.

So how do we show our reverence to God? I believe Joshua gave us clues as he followed the ark of the covenant in the third chapter of his journal.

RECOGNIZE THE DIFFERENCE

We show reverence for God when we recognize the distance between the Creator (God) and the created (us). Notice the orders the officers gave the people: "But keep a distance of about a thousand yards between you and the ark; do not go near it" (Josh. 3:4). Why would they maintain a space of about ten football fields between them and the ark? To show reverence for God and his holiness.

One of the more challenging Bible passages records the death of Uzzah, who was killed for reaching out to steady the ark of the covenant

(2 Sam. 6:6–7; 1 Chron. 13:9–10). Apparently those transporting the ark had become careless with it, disregarding God's instructions concerning who was to carry it and how it was to be handled. They were treating it like any other piece of luggage. They had become overly familiar with this sacred object.

There is danger in over familiarity. I'm grateful for the opportunity to enter God's presence with confidence because of Jesus Christ. I celebrate that I can call out to him with the words, "Abba, Father." He is my heavenly Father, but he is heavenly—and I am earthly.

Many people have reduced God's stature to the point of treating him as if he's just one of us. He's our big buddy. In the words of one song, "We pat God on the back like a buddy from out of town." In the process, many have concluded that God, like a genie in a bottle, exists to meet our needs.

Spiritual leaders should model an attitude of submission and reverence for God. In our prayers and in our references to God, it should be obvious that he is God and we are not. In the process of developing an intimate relationship with him, we must not forfeit our reverence for him.

SEEK A PERSONAL EXPERIENCE

We show reverence for God when we seek our own experience with him. Joshua told the people, "Consecrate *yourselves*, for tomorrow the LORD will do amazing things among you" (Josh. 3:5, emphasis added). Joshua wanted them to understand that this movement of God was not just about conquering the Promised Land. It was about expanding their vision of God and deepening their commitment to him.

The same is true for us anytime God does something on our behalf. God is not nearly as interested in changing our circumstances as he is in changing us. He wants us to know him as the God of the miraculous, the one who does "amazing things," not as just the God of maintenance, the one who does ordinary things. Our consecration is a prerequisite to our experience with God.

Undoubtedly, people have heard and told stories of God's intervention in the lives of their parents and grandparents, but each successive generation must personally encounter the power of God for itself. Christian faith is not a hand-me-down, second-hand experience. Yesterday's experiences with God are not enough for today's generation.

Spiritual leaders must ensure that their young people are encountering the same amazing God they know. This is often thwarted by the false assumption that today's generation will experience God in the same way previous generations did. We preserve past methods and means rather than focusing on the desired outcome—that the new generation would know a God who does "amazing things" among them.

Our Saturday night service was up tempo and casual. When a dear older saint decided to visit the Saturday evening service, I warned her that this worship service might not be for her. She insisted she was pretty flexible and it would be fine.

From the expression on her face when she left, I knew her flexibility had been stretched and snapped. She said nothing, but the next week I received a letter about the "bar room" atmosphere of the service and the lack of "true worshipful music."

Generally, I let a few days pass before I answer such letters. Then I can respond more objectively and the letter writer can hopefully receive my response more objectively. But before I could answer her letter, I heard from her again. This time she said, "I realize that service is not for me. I'll stick with our Sunday morning services."

She was right. We designed that service with a particular target audience in mind, and it wasn't for saints in their seventies.

"As I think back on the service," she continued, "while it wasn't what I would consider a worship service, the younger people appeared to be worshiping and genuinely seeking God."

Bravo! She was giving the next generation the opportunity to consecrate themselves to God in a way that was meaningful to them. Reverence means keeping an updated relationship with God. If the last thing God did for you was in the good old days, your relationship with God is a matter of remembrance rather than a matter of reverence.

LOOK FOR EVIDENCE OF GOD'S WORK

We show reverence for God when we see evidence of God at work. "This is how you will know that the *living* God is *among* you and that he will certainly drive out before you [the people occupying the land] (3:10, emphasis added). They would know God was among them because they would see evidence of him at work.

It is an act of worship to look for evidence that God is alive and well. One of the ways we do this is to notice when God answers our prayers and then give him the credit for it. So often we ask for something from God, he does it, and we move on to our next request as if we are oblivious to what he has done.

A key dimension of Kentwood Community Church's ministry was small groups. This fellowship opportunity was offered nearly every day of the week. Groups met at a variety of times and places. They incorporated into their meetings a time for the sharing of needs and prayer. Many of the groups took it a step further. Not only did they make prayer requests, but they also recorded those requests in a journal. They reviewed the requests to see if there had been answers to prayers and then celebrated what God had done. That is an act of reverence—seeing evidence of God at work. It is something that should be a part of the Christian life in times of personal devotions as well as in public worship. We are irreverent when we take God for granted; we show reverence when we notice what he has done and thank him for it. It also reminds us that we serve a God who is alive and well.

LIVE IN OBEDIENCE

Finally, we show reverence for God when we live in obedience to God's commands. "So when the people broke camp to cross the Jordan, the priests carrying the ark of the covenant went ahead of them" (3:14).

Obedience is the ultimate test of reverence. No amount of worship is a substitute for doing the will of God. King Saul found that out when he disobeyed God and attempted to compensate for it with a hastily convened offering of sacrifices. Samuel confronted him with the words,

"To obey is better than sacrifice" (1 Sam. 15:22). The Lord still "detests the sacrifice of the wicked, but the prayer of the upright pleases him" (Prov. 15:8).

Do churches sometimes substitute worship for obedience? Do they pray earnestly and publicly for lost souls, but make little effort to reach the lost in their community? Do they sing "Faith Is the Victory" with gusto, but pursue only risk-free ministry? Do they vigorously discuss passages such as Ephesians 5:29–32, only to leave the room to gossip and let conflicts with others remain unresolved? If they do, their worship shows no reverence for God.

In fact, many people substitute an experience of worship for "moving out" when God tells them to move. They shed a few tears and feel emotionally relieved—as if that will be an answer for the conviction of God's Spirit they feel. They put a few bucks in the plate as if to bribe God to change his mind. They feel their time in church will be an acceptable trade for the time God wants them to spend influencing their unsaved neighbor. This worship is centered on human comfort, not submission to God.

These are the attitudes and actions of reverence. God is more delighted with these expressions of reverence than with those that are merely a formality.

OUR FOCAL POINT

We no longer follow the ark of the covenant, but we are not left to wonder what our ultimate focal point should be. "Let us *fix our eyes* on Jesus, the author and perfecter of our faith, who for the joy set before him endured the cross, scorning its shame, and sat down at the right hand of the throne of God" (Heb. 12:2, emphasis added).

Jesus came from heaven to earth, living a life offered in obedience to God's purposes. He is a reference point we can relate to, one who fully entered into our humanity. Yet we owe him our reverence and allegiance, for he ascended from earth to heaven and has assumed again his rightful place of authority at the throne of God. We set our minds and hearts on things above (Col. 3:1–2), so that our lives and churches might be available to him.

7

DON'T STOP NOW

Joshua 3:1-17

Momentum Builder	Momentum Buster
Momentum is developed by moving ahead even when obstacles remain.	Momentum is drained by succumbing to the paralysis of analysis.

Because I am a pastor, people seek my counsel for a variety of reasons. Most often, they request guidance in finding God's will for their lives. They may be in a crisis and want to know God's way out. They may be experiencing a significant change and wonder where God wants them to go next.

Knowing God's will is a theologically complex issue, but most times, the steps in pursuing it are fairly simple. I frequently lead those I counsel through a series of questions such as:

> "Once a man understands an idea, he can identify with it, acknowledge it and make it his own."
>
> —ARISTOTLE

- How is your relationship with God?

The majority of God's will relates to who we are, not what we do. He wants us to walk in fellowship with him. I'm convinced this is part of the reason God does not drop a blueprint of our future from heaven—we'd depend on the blueprint rather than upon him.

> "But one thing I do: Forgetting what is behind and straining toward what is ahead, I press on toward the goal to win the prize for which God has called me heavenward in Christ Jesus. . . . Join with others in following my example, brothers, and take note of those who live according to the pattern we gave you."
>
> —PHILIPPIANS 3:13–14, 17

- Are you living in obedience to God?

Sin hinders our communication and relationship with God. If we have not done what God has already shown us to do, it's not very likely he'll continue to show us what he has in mind for the future. God is not in the business of satisfying our idle curiosity, or of giving us the whole picture so we can decide whether or not we want to buy into his plan.

- Have you prayed about it?

This seems like an obvious question, but I'm continually surprised by the number of people who talk to everyone but God about what his will might be for them. Prayer can be hard work, and many detour around it by asking a pastor or a lay leader for advice instead of praying about it themselves.

- Have you weighed the options?

Most times, when the above three questions are satisfactorily answered, God expects us to use our sanctified common sense. He often works through the desires of our hearts and the reasoning of our minds to reveal his direction. Identify the options and weigh the pros and cons of each option. When this is done prayerfully, it can be a source of great insight.

Once I've reviewed these questions with the people I counsel, I advise them to get moving in a particular direction. I suggest that as they prayerfully move forward, they ask God to close the door if they are headed toward something other than his will. In the words of Henrietta Mears, "You can't steer a parked car." You do the moving; let God do the steering.

I've discovered that when people are experiencing a change, they instinctively slow down. Decision-making has a certain inertia built into it. People can become more committed to protection of self and their interests, opting for the path of least resistance rather than the path that offers the greatest progress. Or, they will endlessly review the options before proceeding, allowing the paralysis of analysis to take hold.

Part of the task of leadership is to reverse that trend, to create a sense of urgency. Leaders invest their credibility to help people overcome the lethargy that can set in. As leaders help to get the ball rolling, this momentum gives commitment a chance to flourish. Wise leaders understand the dimensions of momentum, the process by which people become part of a movement of God.

That's exactly where we find Joshua and the people as we revisit chapter 3 of his journal. All the preparations had been made to enter the Promised Land. All that needed to be said had been said, and all that needed to be done had been done. It was time to cross the river. Joshua understood the dynamics of spiritual movement. He didn't yell, "Everyone into the river!" expecting all to move out at the same time. He orchestrated the transition according to principles that are equally relevant to the people of God today.

THE RIPPLE EFFECT

Have you ever thrown a pebble into the calm waters of a pond? When the pebble hits the water, the ripples begin to radiate from the point of impact. This is a picture of how God often works in the spiritual realm.

Joshua's leadership orchestrated a ripple effect. God began the movement in Joshua's heart. Joshua first perceived the change (Josh. 1:1–2), received the vision (1:3–5), and received the challenge to be strong and courageous (1:6–9). He then communicated to his officers (1:10–18) who went throughout the camp preparing the people to break camp and move out (3:2–4). The priests carrying the ark of the covenant were to lead the processional into the Promised Land (3:6). Representatives from each of the tribes were given a special role in the movement (3:12). Finally, all the people were to join in.

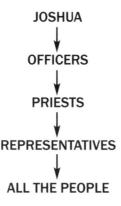

Joshua understood that even though he was pursuing God's will, he needed to align the various sources of influence so that everyone could participate.

A similar ripple effect is seen in many places. In most businesses, influence ripples from the owner to the managers to the employees. In families, there is the generational ripple—from grandparents to parents to children. When a ripple effect transfers godly values and priorities, many people benefit from it. When the momentum leads in a negative direction, there are adverse consequences for many people. That is why it's important to ask the following questions:

- Whose ripples flow into my life? Are those the influences I want to shape my life?

We are influenced by what and who we listen to and watch on the radio, television, computer, and in person. We are responsible to God for the things we allow to fill our minds and hearts.

- Whose lives do my ripples impact? Am I being a good steward of the influence I have on others?

Just as we are to be good stewards of our time, talents, and treasure, we are to be faithful stewards of our influence. It is a sacred trust that belongs to God and we need to carefully manage it.

Church leaders are responsible for monitoring not only the impact of their individual influence, but the rippling effect in the church as well.

Building on what is demonstrated in Joshua, we can plot the ripple effect in a local church.

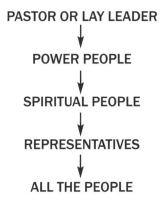

PASTOR OR LAY LEADER
↓
POWER PEOPLE
↓
SPIRITUAL PEOPLE
↓
REPRESENTATIVES
↓
ALL THE PEOPLE

In many churches, just as with Joshua, a vision for ministry begins as God speaks to the heart of an individual. If a church is young, the congregation is large, or the pastor has a long tenure of service, most often, the vision will begin in the heart of the pastor. If the church is small or the pastor is new, it may be a lay leader who gets the ball rolling.

Just as the vision moved from Joshua to his officers, so it also moves from the pastor or lay leader to those who have the power to influence.

While I recognize that it's a bit awkward to discuss power in the context of a church, it is unwise to ignore the reality of it. There are centers of influence in every congregation. Many congregations do not make decisions by congregational vote, but by the reaction of a long-term member or generous giver. If that person's head shakes in disapproval, the vision dies. If that person nods in approval, it moves forward. These individuals or families are sometimes called church bosses. Some use their power very prayerfully and benevolently; others use it selfishly and vindictively. Many churches with dedicated pastors never move ahead because of negative church bosses. To seek their input and support (or at least convince them to remain neutral) can be essential to momentum.

Next, the priests joined in—those with positions of spiritual leadership in the worship activities of the people. Am I saying that there is a difference between the powerful people and the spiritual people in a congregation? Often it's true that those with the most intimate relationship with God are not necessarily the most influential in the congregation. Sometimes that is for the wrong reasons; people who are less spiritual throw their money or weight around. Sometimes it is due to different spiritual gifts; many spiritual people do not have gifts like leadership, administration, and exhortation. They may have a gift like hospitality, which is equally valuable but less visible. But these spiritual people should be sought out to lead the congregation in focusing on the right things as the movement occurs. Just as the priests were to carry the ark of the covenant, so these people are characterized by a reverence for God that is the hallmark of any eternally significant movement.

Then the representatives of the various tribes were given a part in the process. Likewise, churches, especially those that are larger, have various tribes (interest groups). These may be leaders that minister to a particular age group, such as children, youth, or seniors. They may be leaders of classes or small groups. Congregations are often not one big family but a gathering of various subgroups. Attaining ownership of the vision from representatives of various tribes helps build momentum.

Finally, all the people join in. Tragically, this is where many pastors or leaders start. They sense a vision from God then stand in front of the church in a worship service or congregational meeting and announce the will of God for the people. Human nature being what it is, the initial response will usually be resistance. The people feel the leader has sprung something on them and they've had no part in the process. The leader concludes the people aren't interested in God's vision and aren't responsive to the leading of God's Spirit. The problem may not be with the vision or the people at all but with the process. The ripple effect has been ignored.

ORCHESTRATING A RIPPLE EFFECT IN THE LOCAL CHURCH

SEEK GOD'S WILL

Be certain that the ripple effect isn't being employed for selfish or wrong reasons. The process of momentum degenerates into a process of manipulation if God's Spirit is not in it.

IDENTIFY KEY PLAYERS

Who has influence? Who will maintain a godly focus throughout the transition? Have representatives from various groups been included? Most church leaders, with some intentional consideration, can identify these people.

PRACTICE REDUNDANT COMMUNICATION

This means presenting the idea many times and in many ways. Just as ripples in a pond tend to dissipate as they move out from the point of initiation, so a vision blurs as it goes through the process of transmission.

MAKE ROOM FOR RIPPLE CREATORS

I serve with several other pastors on our church staff who are very capable of getting the ball rolling in their areas of ministry. Under the umbrella of a common larger vision, there is room in a growing congregation for many initiating leaders. Many pastors or lay leaders limit momentum because they wrongfully conclude they should only support what they have originated.

CONSIDER DIFFERENT TYPES OF RIPPLE EFFECTS

We're all aware of the negative ones—a prominent member who falls into sin, a family that breaks up, or a gossip who spreads rumors. However, there are also different types of positive and necessary ripples.

Fundraising. Many financial campaigns are designed with initial commitments from the staff and board members, key lay leaders and givers before the congregation at large registers its commitments. The congregation is encouraged by these financial gifts from the leaders.

Spiritual Revival. This happens as God moves first in the hearts of a few, then others, and finally the whole congregation. A sense of anticipation in worship can build as people share with the congregation what God has done for them and what they believe he wants to do for the total church.

Outreach Efforts. Many of the most successful "friend days" have begun by the pastor mentioning the friend he's invited, then board members announcing the friends they've invited, and then key lay leaders announcing the friends they've invited. This gives the congregation a chance to accept the idea and consider those they may want to invite.

These are but a few of the areas where healthy churches experience the ripple effect.

Spiritual leaders must participate in this process. Neutrality is a myth—a leader must exercise appropriate stewardship of influence without developing a spirit of pride. There is no greater joy than fulfilling one's role in a movement of God.

THE THRESHOLD

Between the people of God and the land God had promised them flowed the Jordan River. The time had come for the leaders to step in, and as soon as their feet touched the water's edge, Joshua predicted the waters would part. "And as soon as the priests who carry the ark of the LORD—the Lord of all the earth—set foot in the Jordan, its waters flowing downstream will be cut off and stand up in a heap" (Josh. 3:13).

What Joshua predicted came true as the people of God moved out. "Yet as soon as the priests who carried the ark reached the Jordan and their feet touched the water's edge, the water from upstream stopped flowing" (3:15–16). The miracle was dependent upon their willingness to step in and cross the threshold.

Between every promise of God and its fulfillment lies a river that will test the faith of spiritual leaders. It is an obstacle to overcome. And obstacles cause people to balk.

There are multitudes of people who know where they are in life and also know what God has promised them. But they are stuck at the edge of the river—unwilling to step in. Many tremendous people are mediocre Christians because they lack the willingness and faith to cross the threshold. It is the difference between knowing what decision to make and having the courage to make that decision.

In the same way, many churches go only to the river's edge and no further. It's not that they don't know the promises of God—in fact, these churches may be full of people who pray fervently and study Scripture diligently. But they are intimidated by a threshold—financial, organizational, or spiritual. Inertia sets in, the years go by, and the ministry dies a slow death.

Over the years, Kentwood Community Church encountered many thresholds. During these times, the simple growth everyone enjoyed was replaced by what distinguishes the truly committed—sacrificial growth. In broad strokes, I trace the church's history in this way.

SACRIFICIAL GROWTH

During these years (1979–1983), we met in rented facilities with no guarantees that our new church would survive. The inconveniences and challenges ensured that everyone who joined us did so because they believed in our vision and had faith in our future. Numerical growth, however, was very slow during this time.

SIMPLE GROWTH

We moved into our first new facility, and people joined us by the hundreds. Some came because they believed in the vision, some because of the programs, and some because they liked our new little church building. For the first time, we had a significant number of people who were just spectators, who did nothing more than attend. Growth was simple in this time period (1983–1985), not requiring much commitment from those who attended. It was easy to be part of the church during this time.

SACRIFICIAL GROWTH

We began the process of relocation from our six-and-a-half-acre site to our fifty-acre site. This transition period (1986–1987) fostered a new level of expectation for financial and ministry involvement. Some people left, feeling they were losing the church they had enjoyed. For those who remained, however, there was greater ownership in the vision and a blossoming of new levels of commitments.

SIMPLE GROWTH

With relocation complete, we overcame the initial discomfort of being in new facilities. During this period (1987–1992), we grew rapidly in attendance and had new visibility in our community. People wanted to be part of the church where things were happening and momentum was building. It was simple to enjoy what God was doing and to slip in and slip out of services.

SACRIFICIAL GROWTH

We began discussing a new sanctuary project and raising funds for it (1992–1996), but had not yet moved in. The size of the facility and the finances it necessitated tested our commitment to reach our community for Christ. Again, people left and attendance growth peaked. People were counting the cost of being part of the church's future and determining whether they were willing to sacrifice personally to invest in it.

SIMPLE GROWTH

We completed our new sanctuary, the Celebration Center, and saw hundreds of people filter through to check it out (1997–1998). It was more beautiful than imagined, especially in comparison to the plain, multipurpose room we had worshiped in for the previous ten years. We also had excess seating because we decided to continue our Saturday evening service and only reduce our Sunday morning schedule from three services to two (instead of one). There was room for everyone in this wonderful worship space.

SACRIFICIAL GROWTH

It became apparent that the plateau we were on before moving into the new Celebration Center was continuing (1998–2003). We had to face the painful reality that it wasn't facilities alone that had constricted our growth. It's easy to blame facilities because no one takes it personally. But we began the painful process of exploring necessary changes in personnel and programming. We had to do a heart check: Would we simply celebrate what God had done in the past and rest on our laurels? Or would we sacrificially make the necessary changes in order to be part of what God wanted to do next in our church and community. This sacrificial growth time is explored more fully later in this book.

While there were other thresholds along the way, these were the major defining moments in the church's history. If you were to plot your church's history according to periods of simple growth and sacrificial growth, how would it look? If you were to plot your personal spiritual history, where would you see the thresholds of commitment?

Here are some observations from those times at the river's edge, those moments that require faith to step in and take a risk to be part of what God is doing:

- Many people come during times of simple growth, just as great crowds followed Jesus to witness his miracles and listen to his parables. But their level of commitment is unknown until the church enters a period of sacrificial growth.
- People who do not stay with a church during a sacrificial time are not necessarily less spiritual or less committed. It may simply be the first time they are grasping the church's vision and don't feel led by God to be part of it. When sacrifice is required, people become more

thoughtful about the future and whether that future is one they will choose. Be careful about speaking in derogatory terms about those who leave; departure may be God's will for them.

- People who leave during a sacrificial time may return when the simple growth phase returns. Some people who left when we were anticipating relocation returned after relocation was complete. They watched things happen rather than taking part in the happening.
- Sometimes people are uncomfortable with a threshold the church is crossing because they are simultaneously crossing a personal threshold. They may be overwhelmed with a family situation or career transition. They may have all they can do to cross that threshold, let alone be part of the move the church is making.
- Spiritual life and character are deepened during the sacrificial growth, not the simple growth periods. That is true of individuals and of churches. It is sacrifice that tests the fiber of a pastor, lay leader or congregation. It's amazing how many pastors feel called by God to move elsewhere when they sense that simple growth is ending and sacrifice lies just ahead. Lay people sense that same call. This leaves churches on plateaus and people in shallow walks of faith.

Crossing a threshold requires faith, and Joshua demonstrates the courageous faith necessary to move forward. This section of the book of Joshua reveals two stages of faith:

- The "Say It" Stage: Joshua announced what God was going to do (Josh. 3:13) before God performed the miracle. Joshua had the courage to hear from God and then communicated the promises of God to his people. It takes courage to publicly commit to a future you believe God has provided before other people witness God at work.
- The "Step In" Stage: The hearers took action on what had been heard and communicated. All that needed to be said had been said; it was time for faith to go to work.

The threshold involved risk and the investment of Joshua's credibility as a leader. Once the threshold was crossed, however, his credibility was greater than ever before. God exalted him in the eyes of the people so they would know he was with Joshua like he was with Moses (3:7).

A threshold is a defining moment. It separates those who are excited about the concept from those who will embrace the commitment. When was the last time you got your feet wet? When was the last time your church stepped in to a significant test of faith?

THE ADOPTION CURVE

Spiritual leaders are crucial to the start of a movement of God, so their ripples of influence encourage others. They also take the lead in stepping in when there is a threshold of commitment to be crossed. But there is another dimension of momentum—standing firm until the test of faith passes. "The priests who carried the ark of the covenant of the LORD stood firm on dry ground in the middle of the Jordan, while all Israel passed by until the whole nation had completed the crossing on dry ground" (3:17).

The steadiness of the priests must have encouraged those whose faith wavered as they crossed the river.

Undoubtedly, the people passing through had their doubts and concerns. Some were probably thinking, "With my luck, as soon as I step in the river bed, the wall of water will give way." The next chapter of Joshua gives us a humorous glimpse of their apprehension.

Now the priests who carried the ark remained standing in the middle of the Jordan until everything the LORD had commanded Joshua was done by the people, just as Moses had directed Joshua. The people *hurried over*, and as soon as all of them had crossed, the ark of the LORD and the priests came to the other side while the people watched. (Josh. 4:10–11, emphasis added)

I can picture the people walking slowly to the water's edge, almost dragging their feet. Then they make a mad dash across the river bed.

Once on the other side, they probably slowed their pace again and acted as if crossing the river was no big deal. Like many of us today, the Israelites were willing to cross the threshold but they sure weren't going to linger there.

The priests stood firm. Some people who crossed the river that day probably did not have great faith in God. They might not even have been excited about the Promised Land. The desert was just fine for them. They had the courage and willingness to cross the river, however, because when their faith wavered (or maybe had not yet developed), they saw their spiritual leaders standing firm.

Years ago, while doing doctoral studies on change management, I first came across a formidable field of research on the diffusion of innovation. Fortunately, its basic premise has been reduced to simpler form and has become popularly known as the adoption curve. The adoption curve validates something we all have observed. Some people are more open to change than others. Some welcome change and even get restless when it is not taking place. Others—more committed to the status quo—resist change. In churches, people are located at various points on this change continuum:

CHANGE CONTINUUM

Open			Resistant
Early Adopters 10–20 percent	Middle Adopters 60–80 percent	Late Adopters 5–20 percent	Never Adopters 2–20 percent

Aubrey Malphurs and others give us some additional insights into these groups:

- Early adopters generally make up 10–20 percent of a congregation. Their motto is "believing is seeing," and they adopt new ideas quickly. They are not only open to change, but also get restless if some changes aren't happening. They may even create change for change's sake in situations where it is not warranted.

- Middle adopters make up the majority of most churches (60–80 percent). Not quick to accept new ideas, they initially offer resistance. However, once they have time to think about a worthwhile change and see the commitment of others to it, they hop on board and actively support the initiative.
- Late adopters comprise 5–20 percent of a local church. They resist change, holding to the motto "seeing is believing." Only after the vast majority has actively embraced the change are they willing to go along. Even then, they may simply acquiesce to what is happening and lobby for a return to the way things were if the change process stumbles.
- Never adopters (2–20 percent) will not embrace change no matter who is for it and how worthwhile it turns out to be. They'll drag their feet into eternity—committed to the past and backing into the future.[1]

As I've looked at our church and briefly glimpsed the experience of other churches, I've made these observations:

- The longer a church has been around and the longer it has been since changes have been made, the more the church membership is found on the right side of the continuum. There are more middle and late adopters and fewer early adopters. Conversely, the newer a church is, or the more frequently it has experienced change, the more the church membership is found on the left side of the continuum. This is part of the reason newer churches are more flexible than older churches.
- Which types of adopters are selected for leadership says a lot about a church. Churches longing for stability resist placing early adopters in places of influence, while churches aiming for increased creativity and flexibility often seek out early adopters as leaders.
- How open a person is to change is more a reflection of experience and personality than of spiritual maturity. Leaders must resist the tendency to label certain people as spiritual or carnal based on their response to change.

- Church leaders tend to spend too much of their time with never adopters, who are often the proverbial squeaky wheels that get the grease. To prepare a church for the future, it is much better stewardship of time to invest in early and middle adopters.

Recognizing the various responses to change will help your church strategically involve as many as possible in a movement of God.

How does this relate to standing firm? I believe standing firm allows more people to be part of what God is doing. The middle adopters—and even to some extent, the late adopters—will become part of the change by witnessing the unwavering commitment of others to it. The faithfulness and consistency of spiritual leaders as times passes allows more people to get on board and acquire ownership of the vision.

Anyone who has been a spiritual leader knows that transition times make people nervous. People will seek out leaders to discover whether or not they are really committed to the new direction. If the leaders waver in their commitment, people may refuse to accept the change. If the leaders are consistent in their commitment, the people's nervousness begins to dissipate and resistance fades. People are watching, and a spiritual leader's firm stand helps them take new steps of faith.

8

A LEGACY
WORTH FOLLOWING

Joshua 4

Momentum Builder	Momentum Buster
Momentum is developed by creating a lasting legacy.	Momentum is drained by settling for superficial success or being satisfied with the past.

Measuring success is a baffling exercise. Everyone has a different perspective on what represents a successful person or organization. Christian leaders find it even more complicated, for the ultimate criteria is not found in the realm of man but in the eternal judgments and rewards of God.

> "May all who come behind us find us faithful. May the fire of our devotion light their way."
> —JON MOHR

HOW A LEADER EVALUATES SUCCESS

HISTORY

Upbringing and past experiences influence one's view of success. Many adults still live to please their parents and will not feel successful until their parents are satisfied. Many church leaders compare their present church with the one in which they were raised or the church they first attended after their commitment to Christ. They determine success through a historical reference point.

> "This is what Hezekiah did throughout Judah, doing what was good and right and faithful before the LORD his God. In everything that he undertook in the service of God's temple and in obedience to the law and the commands, he sought his God and worked wholeheartedly. And so he prospered."
>
> —2 CHRONICLES 31:20–21

This means of evaluating success is less than objective because a person's view of history is frequently more a matter of perception than reality. How we remember the past often overrides the actuality of the past. As a general rule, if people feel positive about a past experience, they tend to exaggerate its good. If they feel negative about a past experience, they tend to magnify the bad.

I've been amazed at the gap that exists between perception and reality. Because our congregation was a melting pot of church backgrounds, people at times prompted our church to conform to methods used by a church they'd previously attended. Some who came to our church because we were different from what they were used to would eventually begin to long for the good old days and attempt to change the church to reflect their past. One couple shared with me how great the small group ministry was in their previous church, so I called their former church to learn more about this great ministry. I discovered that it was very similar to ours—but they perceived a world of difference. It is perception, not reality, that influences feelings.

PERSONALITY

Someone with a competitive personality measures success by outperforming another person. Someone who is cooperative associates success with being a team player. A dominant person views success as being able to have everything under control. A highly relational person feels successful when everyone else feels good about what has been accomplished.

At Kentwood Community Church, we assisted our leaders in identifying their spiritual gifts and understanding their personality styles. One year, all church board members completed a personality profile. We laughed when we realized how often our personalities reflected our positions on issues. We also recognized that, while no one can be truly objective, discussion is usually enhanced when people are cognizant of the natural tendencies of their personalities.

PEER GROUP

It is human nature to compare ourselves with people we view as peers. If we are keeping pace with them or doing a bit better than they are, we feel successful. If we're losing ground, we may become anxious and conclude that we've failed.

While I'd like to believe that spiritual leaders never engage in harmful comparison, it is a regular activity in ministerial gatherings and denominational conferences. I've witnessed people who have had a great year of ministry deflate after someone details a year that appears even better. The apostle Paul warns of the danger of comparison in 2 Corinthians 10:12, and Scripture emphasizes that each of us must give an account (Heb. 4:13).

Factors like these make success a highly subjective phenomenon.

THE SUCCESS CONTINUUM

Churches try to evaluate their success, and they should. As I've interacted with pastors and leaders of many churches, I've observed a continuum of success measurement:

Superficial ——————————————————— Spiritualized

While few church leaders are found at the extreme ends of the spectrum, let me briefly describe how those ends might appear.

SUPERFICIAL

In this category, external measurements are the only ones that are necessary. A sense of success rises and falls with the attendance pattern. It inflates with the growth of buildings or budgets. It can be associated with the number of prestigious people who attend the church or with those who have gone out from the church and made an impact in their careers or ministry.

There are many problems in using this category to measure a church's success. For instance, external standards of measurement keep changing. When I was growing up, success was a matter of how many buses the church owned. There was no such thing as small groups. Now, few people talk about their buses, but many talk about the number of small groups in their church. In the Wesleyan denomination, a church with an attendance or membership of five hundred people used to be considered a megachurch. Now, our denomination has several churches that exceed that number in worship attendance. Success is a moving target.

But there are even more serious problems with superficial, external measurements. Attendance growth may be a symptom of novelty rather than ministry. Church budgets may expand by catering to wealthy donors but result in the compromise of biblical standards. Excessive building programs may drain dollars and attention from much more worthy endeavors.

A few years ago, I visited a church in Birmingham, Alabama. It advertised a sanctuary that seated ten thousand people. It was beautiful from the road, but as I pulled into the parking lot, the signs of disrepair were obvious. Entering the facility, I noticed that poor maintenance had resulted in a facility that looked several years older than its actual age. I met with the pastor who explained that he was ministering with a very limited staff and program due to budget constraints.

As his story unfolded, I learned that a previous pastor's "vision from God" had dictated the building of a huge sanctuary. This vision severely strained the church's financial resources. The resulting pressure, along with construction difficulties, resulted in a church split. The pastor left to form a new church down the road with people who were willing to believe in the vision he believed God had given him. Now, the new pastor was enthusiastically leading a struggling congregation to rebuild its ministry in the face of incredible obstacles. That big sanctuary, rather than being a symbol of success, had led to the downfall of that church's mission.

SPIRITUALIZED

People on the other end of the success continuum resist any external, tangible assessments of accomplishment. It is hard to criticize this approach because, on the surface, it sounds so spiritual. It is difficult to argue with such pious platitudes as:

- "God has simply called us to be faithful."
- "If it reaches just one soul, it's worth it."
- "We may be small, but we are spiritual."
- "It's quality that matters to God, not quantity."

There is an element of spiritual truth in each of these sayings. God does value faithfulness in the lives of his people and churches. Jesus himself told the story of one lost sheep (Luke 15:1–7), highlighting the worth of one soul. Christ's ministry often took him away from the crowds, allowing him to spend time with a few who were committed to following him.

However, when a small but spiritual church fails to win one person to Christ in a year's time, some tough questions need to be asked about whether that church is responding in obedience to the Great Commission. If church budgets are stagnant, the question of whether there has been an appropriate challenge to biblical stewardship should be addressed. If attendance is declining while the surrounding community is growing, where is the salt and light of spiritual influence?

The book of Joshua helps us evaluate success from God's perspective. We see in chapter 4 the initial fulfillment of a promise God gave Joshua earlier:

> Be strong and very courageous. Be careful to obey all the law my servant Moses gave you; do not turn from it to the right or to the left, that you may be *successful* wherever you go. Do not let this Book of the Law depart from your mouth; meditate on it day and night, so that you may be careful to do everything written in it. Then you will be prosperous and *successful*. (Josh. 1:7–8, emphasis added)

They had entered the Promised Land, completing the first successful steps in a series of acts of obedience that would lead them to conquer this new territory. Their first instructions from God in the Promised Land led them to construct what I call a success symbol, a memorial to a miracle.

GOD'S SUCCESS SYMBOL

When the whole nation had crossed the Jordan, God commanded Joshua to construct a monument. God gave detailed plans for its creation (4:2–3). Joshua passed those instructions on to the twelve representatives from the twelve tribes of Israel (4:4–7). The representatives carried out the instructions they received from God through Joshua (4:8–9).

A closer look at the symbol gives us insight into what it represented. It consisted of twelve stones, one for each of the twelve tribes of Israel. The stones stood for the unity of the nation of Israel and the participation of everyone in the miracle God had done.

The stones were taken from the middle of the Jordan where the priests had firmly stood with the ark of the covenant. When the people passed by, the ark of the covenant represented God's promises. Selecting the stones from this location would have reminded people of the miraculous presence of God. So, this symbol of success highlighted the participation of all of the people and God's provision for them.

What symbols remind Christians of similar truths today? Certainly there is the cross, reminding us of the successful completion of Christ's mission to the world. God's love and the sacrifice of his Son give all people the opportunity to enter into a right relationship with God.

There is the celebration of baptism, a public act of commitment that symbolizes dying to the worldly self and being raised to new life in Christ.

The practice of Communion symbolizes the substitution of Christ as an offering for our sin. The bread represents his body broken for us; the cup symbolizes his blood that was shed for us. At his command, we receive the elements in remembrance of him.

Symbols are powerful reminders, but they can present problems to Christians. Sometimes people forget the meaning of the symbol or attach the wrong meaning to it. People may worship the symbol rather than the action of God the symbol represents.

Symbols can also cause an inappropriate focus on the past. It is much easier to worship a past movement of God than it is to invest the credibility and energy necessary to be part of a new movement of God.

But when symbols are used appropriately, they help us recall God's faithfulness in providing what we need to live in a way that honors him. The symbol God instructs Joshua to create points to the true measurements of success. These measurements remain valid today in determining the success of a movement of God.

MEASUREMENT ONE: TRANSITIONS IN OBEDIENCE TO GOD

The symbol pointed to the successful completion of a transition that had been God's will for decades. The Israelites had crossed the threshold of the Jordan River, leaving behind a life of desert wandering and embarking on the conquest of new territory for God. They had exercised faith in God and carried out his instructions.

Although transition times can be difficult, making it through them is cause for celebration. It is important to recall defining moments—those times when we knew what God wanted us to do and we did it; and when, because of our willingness and his power, new opportunities were given.

In 1987, the church relocated to its present property. We constructed a multiuse facility with a balance of space for children, youth, and adults. Our rapid growth following that move meant the addition of worship services and educational hours. All age groups felt the strain but none more greatly than our children and youth.

Because we were still in debt from the relocation, we believed it was impossible to add facilities through additional borrowing. So, we constructed facilities to serve our children and youth, raising the necessary funds through a campaign called "To Kids . . . With Love." When we completed this educational wing debt-free, we wanted to acknowledge the generous giving and substantial sacrifice of our people. We also wanted to keep the focus on our children. Our solution was to hang a display entitled "To Kids . . . With Love" in the facility. The display contains the names of the children who motivated us to give, not the donors who actually gave. Every time those kids, who are now adults, enter the building, they see their names engraved in this display—it is a symbol of the congregation's love and commitment to them.

That display is also a symbol of a threshold of commitment for the congregation. At a time when many had already given generously, we stepped up to the challenge, and God miraculously provided. That transition time resulted in more than a building. It resulted in a whole new opportunity to impact the lives of children for Christ.

MEASUREMENT TWO: INVOLVEMENT OF GOD'S PEOPLE

The twelve stones represented the participation of the twelve tribes of Israel in crossing the Jordan River. The crossing was something the whole nation did together, even though two and a half tribes would later return to the other side of the Jordan to live. It utilized everyone's abilities—the officers with their military strategy, the priests with their spiritual ministry, the people who prepared to move the camp into the Promised Land. Everyone celebrated what God had done because everyone participated in what God had done.

The finest successes are those which involve the whole body of Christ. Consider the words of 1 Corinthians 12:14, "Now the body is not made up of one part but of many." None of us is exempt from being a part of what God is doing (12:15–20). All of us need each other; we are not self-sufficient, and we do not individually possess all of God's spiritual gifts (12:21–27).

Spiritual leaders must ensure that they help people discover their spiritual gifts and provide opportunities for the use of them. In some churches, people are left with the impression that they don't have a ministry unless they can teach or sing. But what about the gifts of helps and service? Are gifts of mercy and giving being utilized? What about leadership and administration? Is there a way to involve every person and his or her gifts in a churchwide emphasis?

From the beginning, Kentwood Community Church sought to help people discover their spiritual gifts and then pursue a ministry that utilized those gifts. Early on, we used a program called B.E.A.M.— Believers Enabled as Ministers. Later we switched to some of the newer, more sophisticated programs. At times, we did a very good job of helping people identify their gifts and involving them in ministry, and those were times when our church seemed especially vibrant. At other times, we became busy and fell into the it's-easier-to-do-it myself mentality. When people begin to stand on the sidelines as spectators, it's natural for them to become critical and feel as if they don't belong. That slowly drains the vitality from a church.

MEASUREMENT THREE: CREDIBILITY OF THE LEADERS

True success grants spiritual leaders even greater influence in the lives of their people. Joshua had long been in the shadow of his predecessor Moses, but the successful crossing of the Jordan River and entry into the Promised Land gave new credibility to Joshua's leadership: "That day the LORD exalted Joshua in the sight of all Israel; and they revered him all the days of his life, just as they had revered Moses" (Josh. 4:14). Joshua had been strong and courageous in fulfilling his role to move the people of God forward, and God exalted him.

In any movement of God, there must be leaders willing to humbly risk or invest their credibility. This is an act which serves God's people and gives glory to God. Leaders who are proud focus on what their actions will do for them; those who are humble are more concerned about what their actions will accomplish for God and others. When God sees a spiritual leader humbly but courageously risk personal credibility, he knows he can trust that leader with additional influence. "The greatest among you will be your servant. For whoever exalts himself will be humbled, and whoever humbles himself will be exalted" (Matt. 23:11–12). Joshua's goal was not to be revered like Moses. If it had been, God would probably not have used him. Joshua's goal was to be a faithful leader and let God take care of the rest.

Sometimes, leaders claim success, but a closer look reveals that it has come at the expense of their respect in the eyes of others. This is not to say that people will always agree with the leader's direction, or that they won't ask some tough questions along the way. In fact, between the leader's initial investment of his existing credibility and the gift from God of additional credibility, there is often a period of uncertainty. So, in a way, a measurement of success can't be applied until the movement is completed. As the people look back, do they have greater respect for the leader as someone who courageously obeys God, or less respect for the leader as someone who pridefully does what he wants?

MEASUREMENT FOUR: SPIRITUAL LEGACY TO THOSE WHO FOLLOW

The finest success symbols are those which transform physical, programmatic victories into spiritual legacies. The people had crossed the Jordan River and entered the Promised Land—that was a physical, historical event. The monument reminded them that the event was a miracle of God: God provided a way for his people to experience what he had promised. That pile of stones would remain a part of their spiritual legacy.

God knew the stones would serve as a sign among his people for generations to come. The monument would prompt future generations to ask, "What do these stones mean?" (Josh. 4:6, 21). It would create teachable moments for emphasizing such things as how the "flow of the Jordan was cut off before the ark of the covenant of the LORD" (4:7) and, "The LORD your God did to the Jordan just what he had done to the Red Sea when he dried it up before us until we had crossed over" (4:23).

Several years ago, the church I attended while growing up conducted a financial campaign. My parents, who were still members of that church, believed that building a new sanctuary was absolutely necessary to the future outreach of the church. When the time arrived for financial commitments, they put their treasure where their hearts were—they gave generously.

Because they had arrived at their decision prayerfully and had taken a significant step of faith with their financial pledge, they were asked to share their testimony with others. My dad, a man of relatively few words, spoke from his heart. While I could not be there, others reported to me that he mentioned the pledge might have an impact on his children's inheritance. He felt, however, that the most important thing he could leave his children was not a few more dollars but a legacy of generosity. He wanted his kids to know that financial blessings come from God, and that God should be generously honored with them. By their actions, my parents took a physical victory (success in business) and created a spiritual legacy.

Over the years, in my more sentimental moments, I have driven through my old neighborhood and pulled into the parking lot of my former church. Even though my parents no longer attend the church, every time I see the sanctuary, those words come to mind—legacy of generosity. That building is a sign to me of God's faithfulness to my parents and their faithfulness to him.

MEASUREMENT FIVE: TESTIMONY TO THOSE YET TO KNOW GOD

Many people have mistakenly concluded after reading the Old Testament that God was only interested in his chosen people, the nation of Israel. It is true that God selected them from all the peoples of the earth to demonstrate his love and power. However, his work on their behalf was to be a testimony to the whole world of the benefits of submitting to God and seeking a relationship with him. God placed Israel on center stage, but he knew the world was watching and deciding whether they, too, would follow him. God was not only interested in doing something for his people but, "He did this so that all the peoples of the earth might know" (4:24). Perhaps some would put their faith in him as Rahab did. Others would continue in their allegiance to false gods and resist the living God.

The success symbol not only carried a message for God's people and the generations that followed them, but also for all the people of the earth. A movement of God is successful when it not only blesses and builds the faith of those who already belong to him, but witnesses to those who have yet to know and trust him as well.

MEASUREMENT SIX: REMINDER OF THE POWER OF GOD

The success Joshua and Israel experienced pointed to the power of God: "He did this so that all the peoples of the earth might know that the hand of the LORD is *powerful* and so that you might always fear the LORD your God" (4:24, emphasis added). Success points to the activity and sovereignty of God. If the only conclusion had been that Joshua was a great leader or the people had accomplished something special, it would have fallen short of lasting success.

When the power of God is experienced, it is evidenced by increased obedience on the part of his people. It builds their fear of the Lord, an awesome respect for what God can do. The result is submission to God, which is preparation for what he wants to do through them next. False success says, "Look at what we have done," and rests on the laurels of past accomplishment. True success points to the reality that "the hand of the LORD is powerful" and that we should "always fear the LORD" (4:24). That prepares us for the next chapter of his plan.

9

SLOW BUT SURE

Exodus 23:27–31

Momentum Builder	Momentum Buster
Momentum is developed by looking for the redemptive purpose behind God's patience.	Momentum is drained by failing to understand God's timing.

A few years ago, leaders from across the denomination in which I serve gathered for the launch of Leadership Development Journey. Several speakers offered stimulating insights into effective ministry, leaders cast a compelling vision of healthy leaders and churches, and the initial steps of an unfolding adventure were identified. Between the formal sessions, there were hundreds of hallway conversations in which we processed what we'd heard and discussed how people in various leadership roles should respond.

> "The reason [ninety-nine] out of [one hundred] churches that try to make major transitions fail is that they go too fast."
>
> —DOUG MURREN

Repeatedly, stories were shared of steady progress in building churches that glorified God. As I listened, I was moved to affirm and celebrate what God was accomplishing through them. But more often than not, I heard an apology such as: "I realize that it's not dramatic, but . . ."

> "The Lord is not slow in keeping his promise, as some understand slowness. He is patient with you, not wanting anyone to perish, but everyone to come to repentance."
>
> —2 PETER 3:9

That apology is based on a misconception: If growth is not explosive, then it does not fully honor to God. That notion is a discredit to the way God often chooses to work. When we think that way, we offer others an apology rather than offering God glory for what he has done.

One of the greatest challenges for believers is to comprehend God's timing. As if discerning the content of God's will is not difficult enough, we must also discern the calendar of his will. I call it the timing and trust hurdle. The greater the difference between God's timetable and mine, the greater the faith required. It tests my faith when God moves more quickly than I expect, requiring me to pick up the pace. But the greater test is when God moves more slowly than I expect, requiring me to wait upon him.

This is not a new challenge for believers and leaders. Understanding God's slowness was something the apostle Peter felt compelled to address just a few years after the resurrection of Christ: "But do not forget this one thing, dear friends: With the Lord a day is like a thousand years, and a thousand years are like a day. The Lord is not slow in keeping his promise, as some understand slowness. He is patient with you, not wanting anyone to perish, but everyone to come to repentance" (2 Pet. 3:8–9).

Peter wanted his readers to know that God's perspective on time is not bound by human measurements. He also indicated that we sometimes misread the purpose of God's timing.

God's patience always has a redemptive purpose. His slowness does not indicate a failure to keep his promises. Many of us in church leadership are motivated by God's promises. In addition to the biblical promises that apply to all, we sometimes claim specific promises of ministry fruitfulness. We envision what God has promised to do in reaching the people of our communities and maturing the people of our congregations. When that happens more slowly than expected, we begin to doubt the promises. Instead, we should seek to discover God's redemptive purpose.

It is important not to confuse leadership paralysis on our part with God's patience. There have been times when, rather than move at the speed God intended, I've been slowed by fear, discouragement, or laziness. I never want to misrepresent my tardiness as waiting on God. I've had to repent of the times when God wanted to do more with greater momentum, but I disobediently dragged my feet. Now, every time it seems God has slowed down, I check my heart, mind, will, and emotions first.

However, I don't want to compound the paralysis by overanalysis. Even the apostle Paul recognized that some issues of responsibility aren't fully resolved this side of eternity (1 Cor. 4:1–5). Most conscientious church leaders are too hard on themselves and risk being crippled by self-recrimination. Once I've searched my heart, finding forgiveness and learning lessons, I return my focus to the heart of God.

Yes, I have moved slower than God expected. But he has also moved slower than I've expected. If I spend my time wringing my hands and wondering why, I squander the opportunity to join him in the redemptive purpose of his patience. The critical factor in redeeming these slow-motion periods is how I choose to invest the gift of time God has given.

You've heard the saying, "Time heals all things." It's not true. I've seen people use time to become bitter toward God and distant from him. Time heals only if it is invested in pursuing wholeness over brokenness, forgiveness over bitterness. That is especially true for leaders. Time can be spent asking questions that will likely go unanswered, building frustration in the process. Or, it can be invested in building deeper roots, resulting in fruitful ministry. You can redeem the time (Eph. 5:15–16).

GOD PROMISES GRADUAL VICTORY

The Israelites anticipated entering the Promised Land, and God promised to prepare the way. "I will send my terror ahead of you and throw into confusion every nation you encounter. I will make your enemies turn their backs and run. . . . I will establish your borders from the Red Sea to the Sea of the Philistines, and from the desert to the River. I will hand over to you the people who live in the land and drive them out before you" (Ex. 23:27, 31).

Those promises must have engendered a nervous excitement within the people. They were about to see God work in marvelous ways, but they would be required to do their part. These verses reveal the content of God's will for his people.

Embedded between the two verses quoted above is the calendar of God's will. "But I will not drive them out in a single year, because the land would become desolate and the wild animals too numerous for you. Little by little I will drive them out before you, until you have increased enough to take possession of the land" (23:28–29).

This same sense of timing is communicated in Deuteronomy 7:22. While the initial conquest of Canaan would happen quickly, complete victory would be the result of a gradual process. That would allow time for another of God's promises to be fulfilled, for Moses had also prophesied, "He will love you and bless you and increase your numbers" (Deut. 7:13). Claiming the promised territory gradually would prevent the land from returning to a state of natural chaos, as happened later when Israel was depopulated by the exile of the ten tribes to Assyria (see 2 Kings 17:21–26). The gradual conquest would also serve the purpose of casting increased anxiety and confusion into enemy nations as they anticipated their defeat (Ex. 23:27; Deut. 7:23). It is clear that God did not want the Israelites to misinterpret his timetable, taking his slowness as an indication that he lacked the power to fulfill his promises.

The book of Judges lists more reasons why Israel was to inhabit the land gradually. One was that they had violated their covenant with God after the death of Joshua (Judg. 2:20). Their failure to listen to God caused him to say that he would "no longer drive out before them any of the nations Joshua left when he died" (2:21). God also sought to test the Israelites' resolve to honor the covenant and conquer the land (2:22–23). This testing would develop the combat skills of those Israelites who had not fought in previous wars (3:1–2).

Clearly, God had reasons for choosing a slow-motion approach to leading the Israelites in conquering Canaan. How might those reasons apply to us as we seek to claim new territory for God today? Let's examine two of them.

SPIRITUAL FRUITFULNESS: A QUALITY ISSUE

One reason for gradual fulfillment of the promise is identified in Exodus 23:29: "because the land would become desolate and the wild animals too numerous for you." God's aim was to prevent the land from becoming unfruitful. Quick victory would decrease the quality of the land. They would acquire much land but of little worth. It would be quantity without quality, volume without value.

Sometimes God moves slowly to ensure quality. He wants our ministries to be spiritually fruitful, not desolate. While we do not fear wild animals, we must never forget that our "enemy the devil prowls around like a roaring lion looking for someone to devour" (1 Pet. 5:8). If we achieve spiritual victories but God doesn't indwell them fully, we become more vulnerable to our enemy than ever before (see especially Luke 11:24–26). Sometimes God works gradually to improve the quality of the result.

Does explosive growth always decrease quality? No. Many ministries grow dramatically and stay healthy. Yet a human body that grows dramatically after it has reached maturity is likely to be adding fat, not muscle. It takes time and effort to build muscle. Fat can be added very easily. It can be the same way in ministry.

When I look back at some of the explosive growth at Kentwood Community Church, I realize that we were adding fat and not muscle. The body (the body of Christ, of which our local church is a part) was growing bigger but not stronger. The people we added were not contributing to the mission; they were spectators, observing the increasingly exhaustive efforts of those who labored to keep pace with their demands. We developed some of our greatest weaknesses during the go-go years, and some of our greatest strengths in the slow-growth years.

Here are a few of the ways God's gradual moving allowed us to strengthen our leaders and our church.

TIME TO MONITOR HEALTH

Slow-growth times have allowed us to monitor the health of our congregation. On an annual basis, our church completes the Natural Church Development (NCD) survey.[1] This instrument is designed to measure the characteristics of a healthy church, which are:

- Empowering leadership
- Gift-oriented ministry
- Passionate spirituality
- Functional structures
- Inspiring worship services
- Holistic small groups
- Need-oriented evangelism
- Loving relationships

The key to each characteristic is the modifier. Every church has leadership, but is that leadership empowering others or hindering them? Every church conducts ministries, but are people in those ministries serving according to their gifts or simply filling slots in a program? Each characteristic of church health is measured by its adjective.

While each characteristic is vital for a healthy church, and the goal for every congregation should be increased vitality in each area, it's impossible to improve in all eight areas simultaneously. The evaluation helps by directing attention to the minimum factor—that characteristic that ranks lowest. The NCD survey illustrates the quality characteristics of a church as the staves, or slats, of a barrel.[2] When the staves of a barrel are of uneven height, the barrel will leak at the top of the lowest stave. Likewise, if the characteristics of a church are of uneven quality, the church's overall health will never rise higher than the lowest characteristic—the minimum factor. Raising the minimum factor allows a church to release a greater share of the potential God has placed within it, and it increases the likelihood of both spiritual and numerical growth.

The first year Kentwood Community Church took the survey, our minimum factor was functional structures. This factor indicates the clarity of the church's mission, vision, values, and goals. It also reflects the degree to which organizational structures are aligned with the mission, vision, values, and goals.

When the survey revealed that this was our minimum factor, I responded as most pastors do—with denial. How could this be? I had led seminars for other church leaders on vision casting and leadership development. This simply wasn't possible, or so I thought. Yet after overcoming my self-deception and moving beyond the group-think that made us hope only minor adjustments would be necessary, we went to work.

When a church has been recently launched, work in these areas can proceed rapidly. But when a church is more than two decades old and has structures in place that are less than functional, it's a different story. It took more than a year—and some painful personnel and program changes—to raise this minimum factor.

Attaining health in church life can be a costly and complex process. It takes time, but it's time well spent. God wants his church to be healthy, and while he has little tolerance for time wasting, he graciously allows us to spend time in becoming more vital.

TIME FOR PERSONAL GROWTH

Slow-growth times also allow for the pursuit of personal and professional growth. That's a daunting challenge for any leader. Tragically, many leaders plateau far too early, putting a lid on their personal development as well as their ministry potential. John Maxwell describes this as the Law of the Lid. "Leadership ability is the lid that determines a person's level of effectiveness. The lower an individual's ability to lead, the lower the lid of his potential. The higher the individual's ability to lead, the higher the lid on his potential. . . . Your leadership ability—for better or for worse—always determines your effectiveness and the potential impact of your organization."[3]

Maxwell goes on to share the good news that you can raise the lid by increasing your leadership ability.

Some other leaders cease to be effective because they keep moving geographically rather than personally. When their current ministry situation develops to the point where it stretches their ability, they move on to a ministry that allows them to operate within their comfort zone. While there certainly are times when a pastoral change or move to a new church home by a lay leader may be divinely inspired, such changes can be substitutes for the hard work of stretching leadership ability.

I came to Kentwood Community Church in 1979 as a recent college graduate with no full-time ministry experience. The group of six believers that formed the genesis of the church didn't require much leadership. During my first two years in ministry, my mentor and founding pastor, Dick Wynn, stretched me significantly. Then he left, which stretched me even more by placing me in the role of senior pastor. In the decades since, my leadership abilities have been tested countless times, found deficient, and forced to expand. Did I immediately see my need to grow and instantly make adjustments? Hardly.

Many of those who served in lay leadership roles had been with us for most of the church's history. They began in roles that focused more on doing than leading, roles marked more by simplicity than complexity. But over the years, new levels of leadership had been required of them, and they'd grown to meet the challenges. Those adjustments required the investment of time in learning new skills.

At times, every leader has felt like shouting "Wait for me! I'm your leader!" Ideally, leaders would always learn new leadership skills before they were necessary. Realistically, we identify the need for those abilities only when circumstances demand them, then work to catch up to those demands. God graciously moves slower at some times to allow leaders to come in step with his plan.

We have a God who loves to cause people and leaders to grow. He wants us to be part of what he will do next, not only what he did last. He comes alongside us and—with either a kick to the backside or an arm around the shoulders—moves us forward. It may seem painfully slow at times, but looking back, we can see that progress has been made.

TIME TO LIVE BALANCED LIVES

God wants us to live balanced lives. He sometimes moves slowly to give us time to grow as leaders, but he wants us to remain healthy in that process. If all that were required of us was leadership development, perhaps the pace could be increased. But we are whole people, with physical, emotional, relational, and spiritual needs. We must grow not only as leaders, but also as individuals. And as individuals, we fulfill roles in families, neighborhoods, communities, and, most of all, in the body of Christ. That makes life a balancing act.

Our culture celebrates one-dimensional success. We admire the athlete who puts the rest of life on hold in order to reach for the gold. We envy the businessperson who climbs over everyone and everything to ascend the corporate ladder, winning increasingly impressive titles and salaries. We applaud the celebrity who readily sacrifices family on the altar of fame.

I will stand before God someday not only as a leader, but also as a husband, father, son, and friend. He will assess my stewardship of money, time, and talents. He will also evaluate my management of physical, emotional, and mental health. He'll look inside my soul. On that day, I want to hear, "Well done, good and faithful servant."

In late 1984, I made a commitment to live as a whole person. Realizing my inability to accomplish that on my own, I established an accountability partnership with a trusted friend. We have met every other week for the better part of two decades, sharing our dreams and reinforcing our disciplines. Annually, we've tweaked our list of accountability goals to help us develop more fully in all dimensions of personal life and in all relationships that we value.

I coauthored a book called *Accountability: Becoming People of Integrity* to help others learn how to establish accountability partnerships.[4] At that time, I expressed the conviction that nothing I had done on a purely human level was more beneficial for my well-being than the establishment of this accountability relationship. That conviction has stood the test of time.

Would it be more efficient to live life one-dimensionally? Yes. Is it more eternally significant to live life multidimensionally? Absolutely. There are times when the values of efficiency and eternity collide. Eternal values are always preferable. Life may progress a bit more slowly at those times but much more fully.

TIME FOR CULTURAL CHANGE

Gradual growth allows time for cultural change, not just circumstantial change. Put another way, it's one thing to modify a program; it's quite another to transform a person. Even more difficult is to transform a church full of people.

Let's suppose that we want to imbed evangelism deeply into our church's culture. We might choose to lead a training course, such as Becoming a Contagious Christian based on the book with the same title.[5] Or, we might hold special evangelistic events and encourage members to invite unchurched people from their sphere of influence. We could encourage each member to develop a list of people they love who do not have a personal relationship with Jesus Christ and pray for them regularly.

Would one class, event, or prayer list create a church that has a heart for the lost and prioritize its ministries of outreach? No. It would take repeated seminars, events, and prayer times—as well as modeling by the leaders, testimonies of life change, and messages from the pulpit—to cause an evangelistic heart to beat within the church's culture. It would take repeated emphasis over a period of time.

God sometimes moves slowly so that the things most important to him will become the things most important to us. Most churches have seen a number of fads come and go. Longtime church members usually develop an initial resistance to any new emphasis, marked by "this too shall pass" skepticism. Perseverance is the only way to overcome this. As weeks fade into months, it will become clear that the new emphasis is not a fad but a significant change in the church's value system.

The Bible is clear about the role of perseverance in the development of an individual's character (Rom. 5:3–4). Perseverance is also critical to the development of a church's character or culture. God's patience and our perseverance contribute to producing lasting change. The change must become part of who we are, not just something we do.

I enjoy watching football on television. One of the things that makes a game interesting is slow-motion replay of important events. After a touchdown catch, for instance, the director will break away from the live action to show a replay of the score in slow motion. It's amazing what you can see in slow motion that you miss at full speed. Slow motion has a way of revealing what really happened so that it becomes obvious which actions were important and need to be maximized and which were futile and need to be discarded.

So it is with slow-motion times in ministry. God may intentionally slow down development so that leaders can see what is really happening and adjust accordingly. He doesn't want us to miss anything, including the qualities that will increase our spiritual effectiveness.

SPIRITUAL FITNESS: A QUANTITY ISSUE

Another reason that God sometimes moves slowly is identified in Exodus 23:30, where Moses stated that God would not allow the Israelites to conquer the land "until [they had] increased enough to take possession of the land." God was concerned about their capacity to populate the Promised Land. Sometimes God moves slowly to allow us to acquire the necessary spiritual fitness to fully possess his promises. It's a capacity issue.

The most common measurement of quantity in the church is attendance. When we think of capacity, we may think of the seating capacity of the church building. Those are visual, and sometimes helpful, quantitative measurements. But there are other issues that relate to quantity in the church.

LEADERSHIP QUANTITY

For a ministry to move forward, the quantity of its leaders must increase. Different ministries, by their very nature, require different numbers of leaders. In some public meeting rooms, it's required that the legal capacity of the room be posted. I wonder if it would be helpful for some ministries to post their necessary leadership capacity. During periods in Kentwood Community Church's history when attendance was increasing rapidly, it was quite easy to keep up with the challenge of increasing worship leadership capacity. We could add hundreds in attendance by simply adding a service. Since each service was a duplicate of the others, we simply asked the existing leaders to come an hour early or stay an hour later. We added hundreds of attendees—but few new leaders.

Consider, however, what it would be like to add even one hundred attendees to a small group ministry. Ideally, you would have a group leader for every ten or so people. Each of those leaders would have an apprentice. Since it's helpful to have a coach for every five leaders, you'd also need to add a couple of coaches. So, adding one hundred people in attendance at small groups might require the identification of at least twenty new leaders, and that doesn't include those who serve in other leadership roles within a group.

That's why small group multiplication requires a greater investment of time and resources than does the addition of worship attendees. When growing rapidly, it is hard to keep up the leadership capacity for small groups. Looking back, I realize that our worship attendance outstripped our small group formation. The result was that we had more spectators in our services who were only loosely connected to the community of the church. The church seemed more impersonal during that period, and since life change usually happens best in small groups, there was less forward progress spiritually.

Many churches try to resolve the capacity issue by adding to the workload of existing leaders. In some ministries, this is workable, but not in most. Kentwood Community Church's children's pastor discovered that the multiplication of leaders was a key factor in retaining existing leaders because placing a greater load on existing leaders increased burnout. When a person is burned out in a ministry, he or she tends to warn others of the danger, causing potential leaders to avoid volunteering in that area. In fact, our children's pastor discovered that it's easier to fill twenty positions that have a reasonable load limit than to fill ten positions that are on overload.

God may cause growth to happen more slowly to allow the leaders to emerge who will adequately staff the ministries required for a healthy church. In the wonderful leadership book *Good to Great*, author Jim Collins comments on increasing leadership capacity in a chapter entitled "First Who . . . Then What." Collins points out a problem that plagues not only corporations but also congregations—that is, defining the "what" of the organization (the mission, vision, and strategies) without defining the "who" (the people who are necessary to reach the goal). Without people, the mission is merely words on paper. Collins makes the point using the analogy of a bus. "If we get the right people on the bus, the right people in the right seats, and the wrong people off the bus, then we'll figure out how to take it to someplace great."[6]

I have used that image as a guideline for my private leadership prayers.

The Right People on the Bus. "O Lord, please draw by your Spirit those people you want to function as part of your body in our local church."

The Right People in the Right Seats. "Help us to prepare them for works of service by identifying their passions, gifts, and personality, matching that to the ministry in which they will experience the greatest fulfillment and fruitfulness."

The Wrong People off the Bus. "Lord, protect us from unfruitful, critical people. As the Gardener (Luke 15), do your work of removing or pruning."

If God wants to take us someplace great, he'll raise the right leaders to get us there and remove those who aren't contributing. But this raising and removing takes time.

OWNERSHIP CAPACITY

A second aspect of quantity is ownership capacity. Slow motion allows time for slower adopters to get on board with needed changes, creating the momentum needed to proceed.

It's amazing the methods God sometimes uses to give the insight necessary for making life change. One day, I struck up a conversation with a pastor whose church had recently completed a building program. The program was controversial because it required the demolition of the original church building. Several longtime members had vocalized their opposition, some threatening to leave or withhold funds if the plan proceeded. In spite of this, the expansion was approved by a congregational vote and the necessary pledges were received.

This pastor, about twenty years older than I and considerably wiser, shared with me some of his experiences as a leader during that event. I asked if the opposition group remained in the church. He said some had left, but those who remained had come to appreciate the new addition and were returning to a more supportive stance toward the church. He went on to say that they were in the process of furnishing the facility, and he was asking those who had not contributed to the building itself to contribute to the furnishings.

It was the reason he gave for this that captured my attention: It was not that the project really needed additional financial support—it had come in well within budget—however, in their initial opposition, these people had gone way out on a limb with their harsh comments. Now, the pastor said, "I'm trying to give them some time to come in off the limb."

His remarks were filled with grace. Many leaders would advocate cutting off the limb and letting the people fall because of their opposition.

142

But grace and time were giving the late adopters an opportunity to be part of what God was doing.

As I mentioned in a previous chapter, some people are initially responsive to change, while others are initially resistant to it. While it's true that you can't wait for everybody—even God won't do that—additional time may allow more people to invest themselves in the new thing God is doing. God sometimes moves slowly in order to increase ownership capacity of a ministry.

REBALANCING

The third way that slow motion affects quantity is that it allows time to rebalance uneven growth. Churches tend to grow unevenly, and perhaps leaders do as well. We don't develop our abilities simultaneously or equally. We make strides in one area, which leaves us scrambling to catch up in others.

UNEVEN GROWTH LEADER

Vision Casting | Confict Resolution | Resource Raising | Strategic Planning

CHURCH DEPARTMENTS

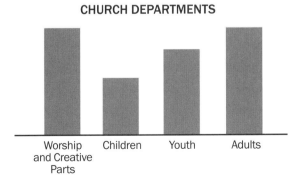

Worship and Creative Parts | Children | Youth | Adults

Uneven development is seen most tangibly in the development of church facilities. Back in 1997, Kentwood Community Church took a big step of faith and built a sanctuary we believed would serve both our immediate and ultimate needs. It was a wonderful facility. It allowed us to retain our single Saturday evening service and return to two services on Sunday morning (as opposed to three or four).

However, if the auditorium had been filled to capacity in our weekend services, we could not have provided the necessary space for children's and youth ministries. We knew that when we built the auditorium, but at the time, we didn't have the resources to provide all the space we would eventually need. So, we did it incrementally. Four years later, for example, we added a student center. The following years gave us the opportunity to rebalance the capacity of our facilities.

Ministries usually develop in an unbalanced way also, since it is very difficult to advance all types of ministry simultaneously. A church may emphasize children's ministry for a while, resulting in an influx of young families to the church. Before long, marriage and family classes will need to be added to the adult curriculum, along with small groups for younger couples and youth ministries for older siblings. About the time those ministries are in place, the children's ministry will need attention again.

Rebalancing takes time. If some capacities are underdeveloped and if that uneven development is exaggerated by explosive growth, the church may become unhealthy. God's patience allows for the rebalance.

I used to meet regularly with the founding pastor of a new church plant in the town where I lived. The church's growth was painfully slow in the initial stages. Like most high-powered leaders, the pastor was chomping at the bit, wondering why everything was taking so long. During the slow time, the pastor used his abundant energy to lead services at his new church as well as speaking at a nearby church that was struggling.

Little did he know that, in God's timing, the members of the struggling church would unanimously vote to close their doors and give their building to the fledgling congregation. The fine, ideally located facility combined with the new church's energy created tremendous momentum for reaching this community for Christ. Was the slow motion of the early days a result of God's orchestrating two churches at different life stages to converge and do something great? I'd say, yes.

We may not always know why God chooses to give victory gradually. I've come to accept that some reasons will remain a mystery. But many of them can be identified and ought to be celebrated. Let us never make excuses or apologize to one another for those times when God moves slower than expected. Instead, let's give him glory and get on with his business.

10

CLARIFYING CORE COMMITMENTS

Joshua 5:1–12

Momentum Builder	**Momentum Buster**
Momentum is developed by renewing your allegiance to God.	Momentum is drained by losing focus.

If I'd been leading the Israelites, my reaction would have been, "You've got to be kidding me! This is neither the time nor the place."

The fourth chapter of Joshua ended with the Israelites' miraculous crossing of the Jordan River. Joshua was exalted and revered (4:14) and the people of the land knew that the Lord is powerful (4:24).

Any leader would have wanted to use the momentum generated by the miraculous crossing to motivate his troops for battle. It had already weakened the enemies' defenses—"their hearts melted and they no longer had the courage to face the Israelites" (5:1). It was the perfect situation for quick action.

> "With the power of conviction, there is no sacrifice."
> —PAT BENATAR

Instead, God decided the time was right for the men of Israel to be circumcised. As I said, my reaction would have been, "You've got to be kidding!"

> "For we know, brothers loved by God, that he has chosen you, because our gospel came to you not simply with words, but also with power, with the Holy Spirit and with deep conviction."
> —1 THESSALONIANS 1:4–5

Crossing the Jordan had removed the last natural barrier between Israel and her enemies. They were officially in enemy territory and vulnerable to attack. Given that the short-term effects of circumcision are debilitating, if circumcision was necessary, it would have made sense to do it before crossing the river.

Why would God make his people vulnerable just as they set foot in the Promised Land? Why would he slow them down when acting with speed seemed likely to bring victory?

When God's action doesn't make sense, that doesn't mean it's a mistake. Usually, it means there's a lesson to be learned.

Earlier, God had promised victory, but gradually. The promise of victory in Exodus 23 is bracketed by commands to worship God alone. God introduces his promise with these words: "Do not bow down before their gods or worship them or follow their practices. You must demolish them and break their sacred stones to pieces. Worship the LORD your God" (Ex. 23:24–25).

God concluded his promise by repeating the admonition: "Do not make a covenant with them or with their gods. Do not let them live in your land, or they will cause you to sin against me, because the worship of their gods will certainly be a snare to you" (23:32–33).

Stated negatively, God's command prohibits expressions of allegiance to other gods. Stated positively, the people are called to worship God and look to him alone for blessings.

There could be no more tangible, personal expression of allegiance to the God of Israel than circumcision. More than a physical act or medical procedure, it was a spiritual act that would position them to be empowered by God to conquer the Promised Land. To undergo circumcision would be a clear sign of their obedience to God.

A SIGN OF REPENTANCE

Joshua 5:4–7 gives the background on why this generation of Israelites had not been circumcised:

All those who came out of Egypt—all the men of military age—died in the desert on the way after leaving Egypt. All the people that came out had been circumcised, but all the people born in the desert during the journey from Egypt had not. The Israelites had moved about in the desert forty years until all the men who were of military age when they left Egypt had died, since they had not obeyed the LORD. For the LORD had sworn to them that they would not see the land that he had solemnly promised their fathers to give us, a land flowing with milk and honey. So he raised up their sons in their place, and these were the ones Joshua circumcised. They were still uncircumcised because they had not been circumcised on the way.

The circumcision of this generation marked the close of a dark chapter in the history of Israel, one of faithlessness and wandering. Now they were to do the one thing necessary to place them in right standing with God. They were no longer uncircumcised wanderers born of disobedient parents but circumcised conquerors. This event was their opportunity to establish a new pattern of obedience in their generation.

The only way to leave behind a sinful past is to repent. God may slow us down to indicate that something needs to be removed from our lives before we can fully embrace his plan for the future. In order to repent, we must overcome the human tendencies toward denial, blame, and rationalization. We'd like to believe that we always respond immediately to God's conviction, but often, we don't repent until he has repeatedly revealed the need for change. Once we do come to grips with his revelation, we must take responsibility before God for our sins of commission and omission.

Over time, Ash Wednesday became one of the most significant services in the annual calendar at Kentwood Community Church. Perhaps that's because repentance is so seldom emphasized in today's celebrative worship climate. This day seemed to tap our longing for some tangible way of showing humility—how else does one demonstrate humility in a public setting without appearing prideful?

The Ash Wednesday service of 2001 marked the close of a difficult chapter in the life of our church. I stood before the congregation as their spiritual leader and confessed the ways in which I had limited the freedom of God's Spirit to work among us. Some of my confessions were things I had done; others were matters I'd left undone. As I looked into the faces of those who felt the impact of my sins and shortcomings, God broke my heart and tears began to flow. His Spirit produced godly sorrow as I read these words: "I, Wayne Schmidt, as senior pastor and team leader for the spiritual health of Kentwood Community Church, have felt led by the Spirit of God to repent of the following sins." One by one I named them:

- Being distracted from my primary calling to provide spiritual leadership.
- Allowing my heart for spiritually lost people to cool, downplaying the fact that hell is a real place and that real people go there.
- Avoiding conflict, allowing tensions and dissension to take root.
- Not praying with the faith and fervency that marked my prayers in the early days of Kentwood Community Church.
- Lacking boldness to declare the truth in love, at times settling for what pleased people rather than what pleased God.

While these sins may not sound as dramatic as moral failure or criminal behavior, they were wrong in God's sight nonetheless. I was careful to avoid grandiose statements that would make the situation sound scandalous while I frankly admitted that my shortcomings had hindered God's work among us. This confession did not lead to a forced resignation, but rather to a new direction.

Following my statement, representatives from our staff and church board led the congregation in a litany of confession. Some of the shortcomings mentioned in the litany had been downplayed or denied for years. Now, they were written down by our leadership team and spoken out by our church family. We sensed that God was honored by our specific, corporate confession. Here is some of what we recited together:

> We have not persevered in developing important spiritual initiatives in evangelism, serving, and fellowship. Instead, we have continually started new programs rather than fully integrating initiatives into the culture of Kentwood Community Church. This lack of perseverance has caused us to keep trying new things while leaving critical areas of church health to die a slow death. We have missed the character development and joy that comes with perseverance.
>
> Our unwillingness to deal with differences and conflict has led to a proliferation of gossip and slander, resulting in division between us. This critical spirit has affected both our fellowship as believers and the witness of the church, dishonoring our Lord Jesus who prayed that we might be one in order that the world may know him.
>
> We have approached worship with a "what's in it for us" mind-set rather than asking "what can we offer to God?" Our preferences have become central, rather than the desire to give him praise. This has made us, mere creatures, the center of attention, rather than our God who is forever to be praised.

Then we used ashes to make the sign of the cross on the forehead of each person who wished to display that mark of personal repentance and humility. Sorrow turned to joy as hundreds of people tangibly indicated their desire that the future be different than the past.

As a congregation, this was our act of repentance, a display of godly sorrow. We could identify with the Corinthians when Paul wrote, "Godly sorrow brings repentance that leads to salvation and leaves no regret, but worldly sorrow brings death" (2 Cor. 7:10). During the remaining Wednesdays of the Lenten season, we met and prayed that we might display the fruit of repentance. Paul wrote, "See what this godly sorrow has produced in you: what earnestness, what eagerness to clear yourselves, what indignation, what alarm, what longing, what concern, what readiness to see justice done. At every point you have proved yourselves to be innocent in this matter" (2 Cor. 7:11). We devoted those prayer meetings to asking God to empower us in each area we'd confessed so that we might "prove [our] repentance by [our] deeds" (Acts 26:20).

Would we have reached that point of repentance as a congregation if we were moving at full speed? While I'd like to think we would have, I believe that the atmosphere most conducive to reflection and confession rarely occurs in a time of momentum. This is not to say that our example is the ideal. In some ways, it's embarrassing to admit that God had to slow us down to a near stop before we acknowledged our sins and shortcomings. It is entirely possible to build in periodic times of reflection, including confession and correction if necessary, so that unconfessed sin does not hinder steady forward progress. That is true both for individuals and for congregations.

In the book *Working with Emotional Intelligence*, the author outlines five characteristics of people who are effective in the marketplace.[1] The first is self-realization, having a conscious awareness of your attitudes and actions so that you know your strengths and weaknesses. The second is self-discipline, having the ability to form new habits. These are integrally linked to repentance. Leaders and congregations need to take time to realize what needs to change and discipline themselves to make those changes.

Immediately after the men of Israel were circumcised, the Lord said to Joshua, "Today I have rolled away the reproach of Egypt from you" (Josh. 5:9). Commentators differ on the exact meaning of this pronouncement. Some believe it is a reference to the fact they had entered the Promised Land, successfully completing their journey from Egypt. Yet since it immediately follows the circumcision, others believe it means that they had finally separated themselves from the last vestige of Egyptian bondage. Whatever its exact meaning, it's clear that God's people had rewritten an old script. They had closed an old chapter of disobedience and opened a new one of obedience. They dealt with the past so they could move unhindered into the future.

A SIGN OF RELIANCE

What makes a leader or a group of people more reliant upon God? If dependence upon God increases effectiveness for God, what kind of environment fosters the greatest level of trust? I'm currently in the process of memorizing passages from John 15, where Jesus described for his disciples that level of dependence that is required for spiritual fruitfulness. Jesus said:

> Remain in me, and I will remain in you. No branch can bear fruit by itself; it must remain in the vine. Neither can you bear fruit unless you remain in me. I am the vine; you are the branches. If a man remains in me and I in him, he will bear much fruit; apart from me you can do nothing. . . . If you remain in me and my words remain in you, ask whatever you wish, and it will be given you. (John 15:4–5, 7)

As followers of Christ, we are to rely upon him for the ability to be effective as a branch relies upon the vine to provide the nutrients it needs to bear fruit.

The ideal condition for creating greater reliance upon God occurs when we simultaneously sense our powerlessness and his powerfulness. That condition is represented by this formula: our powerlessness multiplied by God's power equals a new level of reliance.

That's exactly where the Israelites found themselves. They had just crossed the Jordan River, aided by God's miraculous intervention.

Joshua then told the people why God performed the miracle and why they were to memorialize the moment:

> For the LORD your God dried up the Jordan before you until you had crossed over. The LORD your God did to the Jordan just what he had done to the Red Sea when he dried it up before us until we had crossed over. He did this so that all the peoples of the earth might know that the hand of the LORD is *powerful* and so that you might always fear the LORD your God. (Josh. 4:23–24, emphasis added)

That's one half of the equation—the evidence of God's power.

The other half is their sense of powerlessness. Their circumcision would help create that sense. The fighting men would be incapacitated, leaving them completely vulnerable except for the protection of God as "they remained where they were in the camp until they were healed" (5:8).

After a powerful movement of God, we are often inclined to think we can build upon it. We feel personally powerful because God has shown himself powerful. So, God often chooses those moments to put us in a place where we sense our vulnerability.

One of the greatest challenges of spiritual leadership is the stewardship of power. We usually think of stewardship as managing hard assets—measurable things like money and time. But leaders must manage soft assets as well—things like credibility, spiritual gifts, influence, and power. We become better stewards of power as we recognize that all of it belongs to God and that he can exercise it through the life of any devoted person. He sovereignly chooses to do his work through us, and we are blessed simply to be present when his power is manifested.

Kentwood Community Church often partnered with other churches to reach the community for Christ. Certainly, we were determined to do our part in directly influencing spiritually lost people through the ministries of our congregation. Yet we recognized that new churches are often more effective in reaching spiritually lost people. So, we partnered with other congregations to plant churches. Why are new churches usually more effective in doing evangelism than existing churches? There are many reasons: They're not bound by tradition; they don't have as many power blocks within the church; they aren't as focused on meeting the needs of existing members; and the list goes on. I would add this item: They are more likely to rely on God's power instead of their resources.

When a new church begins, its human resources are extremely limited. Church planters have a big vision and an empty bank account. If God doesn't show up, they won't survive, let alone thrive. But as churches age, they gain resources—members, facilities, programs. They develop the ability to survive for many years whether God shows up or not. There are many churches that are spiritually dead, entirely void of God's Spirit, yet meet every week.

Reflect on your church's history. You may discover that the most fruitful times were when you took the risk of going beyond your resources to rely upon God. When Kentwood Community Church relocated to the current property, not one financial institution was willing to provide the resources that the young church needed. We went out on a limb, accepting a God-sized challenge that stretched every person in our congregation. We all knew that if God didn't show up, there would be no backup plan. We were completely dependent upon him.

More than twenty years later, when we were entering another building program, several banks competed to provide financing, even encouraging us to borrow more than we'd wanted. We could borrow the amount needed to supplement a comfortable level of giving without relying upon God's power. Is that a good place to be? No. It is a very dangerous place to be.

Risk yields reward, and that's especially true when relying upon God. Imagine two circles, one within the other.

God's Power

Our Power

If we live and exercise leadership within the circle of our power, we will be comfortable. We'll always be able to do what we choose to do even if God does nothing. But our circle of influence, the difference we can make in the world, will be limited. We're big fish in a small pond, the pond of our power. When we reach beyond what we can accomplish with our thinking and doing, we take the risk of radical reliance. We enter the realm of God's power. Less comfortable? Absolutely. Will that act of courage make us candidates to witness a movement of God? Undoubtedly.

Tragically, as churches and leaders mature, they operate more within the realm of their power and less within the realm of God's power. The average church plateaus in growth before it is twenty years of age. When does the average spiritual leader plateau in personal growth and effectiveness? By thirty years of age? Forty? A leader's personal power expands as he or she develops new resources—the inner circle grows. But a little more of our power is a sorry substitute for a little more of God's power, which is available only when we take the risk of abandoning our resources to rely on God.

Warning: The risks we take must be acts of faith, not foolishness. They must result from obedience to God's leading. The men of Israel were vulnerable because they obeyed God's command to be circumcised, not because of some rash decision. Vulnerability, by itself, has no value. Reliance that honors God is always a byproduct of obedience.

This issue becomes more complex for leaders when we realize that the method of reliance is just as important as the level of reliance. How much we rely upon God is not the only issue. How we rely on him matters as well. Relying upon God in the future will not require simply more of the same. In the desert, the Israelites relied upon God for food by eating his daily provision of manna. In the Promised Land, God moved them beyond a manna mentality.

On the evening of the fourteenth day of the month, while camped at Gilgal on the plains of Jericho, the Israelites celebrated the Passover. The day after the Passover, that very day, they ate some of the produce of the land: unleavened bread and roasted grain. The manna stopped the day after they ate this food from the land; there was no longer any manna for the Israelites, but that year they ate of the produce of Canaan. (5:10–12)

From then on, Israel would not simply collect food. They had to conquer in order to eat. They had to rely on God at new levels and in new ways. That's the essence of spiritual growth and leadership development.

A SIGN OF RENEWAL

Circumcision was instituted as the sign of God's covenant with the nation of Israel.

> Then God said to Abraham, "As for you, you must keep my covenant, you and your descendants after you for the generations to come. This is my covenant with you and your descendants after you, the covenant you are to keep: Every male among you shall be circumcised. You are to undergo circumcision, and it will be a sign of the covenant between me and you." (Gen. 17:9–11)

By being circumcised, descendants of Abraham indicated their commitment to keep their part of the bargain. God's faithfulness in the covenant is never at issue. He always keeps his word. The question mark is on the human side of the agreement. God looks for our commitment to his work not because he needs us, but because he has sovereignly chosen to work through us. That notion is aptly expressed in the saying, "Without God, we cannot. Without us, he will not."

Circumcision slowed the pace for Israel. The healing process required them to camp until they were healed. While camping, they celebrated the Passover. They had shed their blood to demonstrate their commitment to keeping the covenant. Then they celebrated the Passover, shedding the blood of a lamb as a reminder of God's part in keeping the covenant.

God still requires circumcision as a sign of our willingness to keep his covenant. But there is a new covenant in force.

> "The time is coming," declares the LORD, "when I will make a new covenant with the house of Israel and with the house of

Judah. It will not be like the covenant I made with their forefathers when I took them by the hand to lead them out of Egypt, because they broke my covenant, though I was a husband to them," declares the LORD. "This is the covenant I will make with the house of Israel after that time," declares the LORD. "I will put my law in their minds and write it on their hearts. I will be their God, and they will be my people." (Jer. 31:31–33)

This new covenant, accomplished by the shedding of the blood of Jesus Christ, is what we remember through Communion (Mark 14:24). It's the covenant mediated by Christ (Heb. 9:15).

And this new covenant is signified by a new circumcision. It is a circumcision of the heart. "A man is not a Jew if he is only one outwardly, nor is circumcision merely outward and physical. No, a man is a Jew if he is one inwardly; and circumcision is circumcision of the heart, by the Spirit, not by the written code. Such a man's praise is not from men, but from God" (Rom. 2:28–29).

Circumcision of the heart also involves wounding and healing. The act of circumcision may slow our pace so we can experience the change of heart that God requires.

For Israel, the covenant was the framework for what they believed and how they behaved. It was vital that they renew that covenant before they undertook a task as great as the conquest of Canaan. As leaders and as churches, it is important that we periodically renew our commitment to the beliefs and behaviors that attend our covenant with God.

BELIEFS

It's unfortunate that most Christians exhibit little desire to understand what they believe. Perhaps overreacting to the days when Christians were divided by petty differences, Christians today are all too quick to dismiss any discussion of doctrine as divisive. Their mantra is, "It doesn't really matter what we believe as long as we love Jesus." I support the desire to love Christ with greater intensity, but I also advocate the need to believe in him with greater clarity.

Kentwood Community Church held doctrinal positions that were mostly in common with other evangelical churches. Its distinctive doctrine, however, differed from the dominant Christian belief system in the community. In membership classes, we sought to clearly explain our beliefs. I saw many people in those classes who, without a moment's hesitancy, set aside beliefs they held for decades in order to embrace ours. And I'm not naïve—if they change churches again, they will likely set aside our beliefs to embrace those of yet another church. Doctrines are no longer anchor points for faith but words on paper subject to regular revision.

At Kentwood Community Church, we believed that "fully committed believers live belief-based, value-centered, mission-motivated lives." We encouraged members to examine our beliefs carefully and consider what they personally believed. To prompt that reflection, we added a reflective component to each of our doctrinal statements. Here's an example, taken from the statement on God's Word, the Bible.

We believe that the books of the Old and New Testaments constitute the Holy Scriptures. They are the inspired and infallibly written Word of God, fully inerrant in their original manuscripts and superior to all human authority, and have been transmitted to the present without corruption of any essential doctrine. We believe that they contain all things necessary to salvation; so that whatever is not read therein, nor may be proved thereby, is not to be required of any man or woman that it should be believed as an article of faith, or be thought requisite or necessary to salvation. Both in the Old and New Testaments, life is offered ultimately through Christ who is the only Mediator between God and humanity. The New Testament teaches Christians how to fulfill the moral principles of the Old Testament, calling for loving obedience to God made possible by the indwelling presence of his Holy Spirit.

Do you believe what our church believes?

____ I believe the Bible is God's inspired Word and is fully authoritative in determining the way I should live my life.

___ I believe God's Word is to be trusted more than my thoughts, experiences, and feelings when determining what is best for me.

___ I believe human teaching is to be tested by its compatibility with God's Word.

By adding an opportunity for response to each of our belief areas, we helped people internalize their beliefs.

BEHAVIORS

Our behaviors are the tangible expression of our values. Years ago, I was challenged by a speaker who asserted, "What you value has absolutely nothing to do with what you say." After a pregnant pause, he went on to say, "What you value has absolutely everything to do with what you do." The rest of his unsettling presentation exposed our regrettable tendency to measure spiritual development by talking the talk rather than walking the walk. It's much easier to improve our vocabulary than to systematically incarnate our values in everyday life.

Our need for repentance as a church, and my need as a leader, rose partly from the incongruity that had developed between our stated values and our characteristic actions. Part of the fruit of our repentance was that we spelled out our conviction that "fully committed believers live belief-based, value-centered, mission-motivated lives" by listing the specific values that we hope to exhibit. We ended up with eleven:

- Accountability
- Awareness of and biblical approach to cultural issues
- Biblical communication
- Fellowship
- Growing in relationship with Jesus Christ demonstrated by life change
- Loving one another
- Prayer
- Reaching out to spiritually lost people

- Servanthood through gift-based ministry
- Stewardship
- Worship

For each value, we listed a brief definition along with the Scripture references that provide its biblical foundation. We then created a reflection section that identifies ventures and vampires for each value. Here's how we defined those terms: *venture*—an undertaking involving some risk in expectation of gain; *vampire*—something dead that sucks the life blood from something living.

These words are a bit dramatic, but they reinforce the reality that our actions must either build our spiritual life or drain it. Being aware of what gives life to our values and what sucks life from them helps us to be proactive in making the best choices in any given situation.

As an example, here is how we define the value worship:

We believe that we were created to worship God the Father, Son, and Holy Spirit. We worship God as we come together in public services, in smaller settings, and in private devotional times. We worship God when we submit ourselves to him. The focus of our worship is not ourselves but God. (See 1 Chron. 16:29; Ps. 29:1–2; 63:4–5; 95:1–8; 100:1–2; 135:1–3; Isa. 6:1–4; Luke 4:8; John 4:23–24; Acts 2:42–47; Rom. 1:20–23; 12:1; Eph. 5:19–20; Phil. 3:3; Heb. 10:25; Rev. 4:3–11; 7:9–12.)

VALUE VENTURES

____ I spend time alone in worship—reading God's Word, praying, listening to Christian music, meditating, and so on.

____ I come prepared to enter into times of public worship.

____ I engage in all the dimensions of worship—celebration, reflection, repentance, etc.—regardless of personal preference.

____ I attend public worship almost weekly, making it a priority.

VALUE VAMPIRES

____ I am a spectator and critic, evaluating how well the people up front are doing.

____ I leave a service asking, "Did I like it?" rather than, "What did I offer to God today?"

____ I limit my expressions of worship to the comfortable and familiar rather than seeking what God desires of me.

____ I demean forms of worship that I experience as less meaningful even if others experience them as significant.

By providing a list of ventures and vampires for each value, we offer each member an opportunity to evaluate the degree to which that value is present in his or her life.

Our beliefs and values form the heart of our church's covenant with God. When a company takes its annual inventory, it limits or shuts down other activities. While this temporarily slows productivity, that company understands that an accurate inventory is a tool for evaluating its current condition. Periodically, God will slow down leaders or congregations so they can take inventory to evaluate the current condition of their beliefs and behaviors.

For the people of Israel, the renewal of their covenant with God was a proactive step toward avoiding the temptation to make covenants with the people of the land (Ex. 23:32). So the timing of their circumcision, which symbolized their loyalty to the covenant, was perfect. They were now in the land, seeing firsthand the people who were there and the gods that they worshiped. The renewal of the covenant was a spiritual vaccination that would strengthen their resistance to other gods.

RELEASING GOD'S POWER

The significance of Israel's circumcision might be stated this way:

Repentance + Reliance + Renewal = Release of God's power through his promises

At Kentwood Community Church, one of the ways we lived out the reality of this formula was to seek to reach more people by becoming culturally diverse as a congregation. The population of our neighborhood was about 22 percent minority, while our congregation was about 1 percent minority. Like many aging churches, ours was mostly a drive-in congregation, and we sensed a growing disconnection with our closest neighbors.

We tried to identify areas of prejudice and racism that required repentance. We prayed that God would bring leaders from many cultures to help us reach out to all people more effectively. And we asked God to renew our beliefs and behaviors so that we would genuinely welcome all people. As we were faithful in these areas, we began to witness the release of God's power based on his promise to gather in heaven those from every tribe, language, and people. As we move further beyond ourselves, relying ever more fully on God's power, we're expecting to have a bit of heaven on earth as we worship together.

11

GOD'S POWER FOR GOD'S PURPOSE

Joshua 5:13–15

Momentum Builder	Momentum Buster
Momentum is developed by pursuing God relentlessly.	Momentum is drained by failing to seek God's power.

John Wesley is one of my heroes. Above my desk I've mounted a prayer of his that I believe captures the secret of his success. It's a prayer of yieldedness.

I am no longer my own, but thine.
Put me to what thou wilt, rank me with whom thou wilt.
Put me to doing, put me to suffering.
Let me be employed by thee or laid aside for thee,
Exalted for thee or brought low by thee.
Let me be full, let me be empty.

> "Our power is not so much in us as through us."
> —HARRY EMERSON FOSDICK

Let me have all things, let me have nothing.

I freely and heartily yield all things to thy pleasure and disposal.

And now, O glorious and blessed God, Father, Son, and Holy Spirit.

Thou are mine, and I am thine.

So be it. Amen.

> "The Lord Almighty has sworn, 'Surely, as I have planned,
> so it will be, and as I have purposed, so it will stand.'"
>
> —ISAIAH 14:24

I incorporate Wesley's emphasis on yielding as the exclamation point in my pattern of prayer. My personal prayers generally follow this model:

P — Praising God for who he is and how he works.

R — Repenting of anything that displeases God and resolving to bear the fruit of repentance.

A — Asking, seeking, knocking; persistently pursuing all that is within God's will to give.

Y — Yielding all that I am and have to God's will.

As I yield my life to God at the conclusion of each prayer, I get on my knees (if I'm not there already) in a posture of submission and recall Wesley's prayer of complete abandonment to the purposes of God.

Every movement of God starts in a meeting with God. Every movement of God is sustained by meeting with God. So it's no surprise that after entering the Promised Land, Joshua's first encounter was not with the enemy but with an emissary of God. "Now when Joshua was near Jericho, he looked up and saw a man standing in front of him with a drawn sword in his hand" (Josh. 5:13).

The identification of this man has been the subject of much speculation. Was it a theophany, God appearing in human form? Was it a christophany, Christ appearing in human form? Was it an angel? I think it was an angel. Other places in Scripture record the employment of angels for similar missions. I believe Joshua's encounter with this man and the message he conveyed would have reminded Joshua of his mentor, Moses. God had promised Joshua, "No one will be able to stand up against you all the days of your life. As I was with Moses, so I will be with you; I will never leave you nor forsake you" (1:5).

During his brief time as the point person in this movement of God, Joshua had already had many experiences that paralleled the life of Moses. Moses' commission to Joshua, "Be strong and courageous" (Deut. 31:23), had been repeated three times by God himself (Josh. 1:6–7, 9). The leaders had pledged to Joshua, "Just as we fully obeyed Moses, so we will obey you. Only may the LORD your God be with you as he was with Moses" (1:17). By God's miraculous provision, Joshua had led the people across the Jordan River (3:15–17) just as Moses had led the people through the Red Sea (Ex. 14:21–22).

Now Joshua experienced a holy ground encounter (Josh. 5:13–15) with God. Undoubtedly, Moses had told his protégé the story of his burning bush experience (Ex. 3:2–10). An angel of the Lord appeared to Moses within the flames of a burning bush. His message to Moses began with the words, "Take off your sandals, for the place where you are standing is holy ground" (3:5). That message was almost word for word the same as the message Joshua received from his mysterious visitor (Josh. 5:15).

Was this the angel that God had promised would go before them into the Promised Land (Ex. 23:20–23; also 32:34; 33:2)? If so, Joshua well understood that the people of Israel were to "pay attention to him and listen to what he says [and] not rebel against him" (Ex. 23:21).

THE RIGHT QUESTIONS

Joshua had the presence of mind to ask the man two questions. Much of the wisdom needed for leadership can be found in asking the right questions. When I entered my ministry, I thought that 99 percent of leadership was having the right answers. The more I lead, however, the more I realize that the real task of a leader is to ask the right questions and then carefully listen for the answers. That's true whether I'm seeking wisdom from God, mentors, team members, or seekers. Leading involves focused listening, and good questions bring that focus.

When we're in a hurry, it's hard to listen and easy to jump to conclusions. Slow-motion times can create a context in which we listen to God and others more fully. For years now, I've benefited from the book *Margin*. The author, Richard Swenson, is a medical doctor who identifies four gears in our pace of life.[1]

OVERDRIVE

We operate in overdrive when life's demands require heroic expenditures of energy, causing the release of adrenaline within the body. This gear is intended to be used only on rare occasions, but it is where many people spend the majority of their lives. Running too long in overdrive creates an adrenaline addiction.

DRIVE

Drive is the gear in which we work and play most of the time. Most of the activities of life are enjoyed in this gear.

SLOW

Slow is the gear most conducive to building deep and intimate relationships. Without the rush of adrenaline and activity, we are able to listen more fully.

PARK

Park is a full stop. This is the gear in which we best listen to God. Most people know that, which is why we call our moments of communion with God quiet time. The psalmist speaks often of the power that is gained by heeding God's call to "be still, and know that [he is] God" (Ps. 46:10).

Swenson observes that our society, with its emphasis on productivity and activity, increasingly pressures people to live in drive and overdrive and rarely allows them to operate in slow or park. This has produced a traumatic effect on the relational and spiritual lives of many who are too busy or burned out to develop intimacy with God or others.

If individuals have gears, do churches also? We are energized by the times of dramatic growth and transition that require us to shift into overdrive. But if we live and lead in that gear too long, we may diminish our capacity to sense and obey the leading of God's Spirit. As leaders, if we know we are about to embark on a time that will require us to gear up, we should be especially careful to listen to God. We must be still with God before we speed up for him.

Joshua had some alone time with God's representative just before the battles began. The questions Joshua asked of him zeroed in on the heart of spiritual leadership. The first was the power question; second was the purpose question; both are important.

Kevin Myers, a close friend and pastor of a thriving church in Atlanta, Georgia, teaches that "God's calling is where God's power and God's purpose come together in your life." God gives his power only for his purpose; he doesn't give us his power to pursue our dreams. And God's purpose can only be accomplished with his power. If we try to fulfill God's mission in our strength, we'll burn out long before we finish. The intersection of God's power and purpose causes his kingdom to come and will be done on earth as it is in heaven.

THE POWER QUESTION

Joshua looked up to notice a man standing in front of him. The drawn sword in the man's hand was an unmistakable symbol of power. Joshua's question, "Are you for us or for our enemies?" (Josh. 5:13) was certainly a good place to begin. The man, however, didn't provide a direct answer. He wasn't evasive; in fact, his response was authoritative. He didn't answer this power question simply because it was framed in the wrong way.

Joshua's question made the people of God its point of reference—"Are you for us or for our enemies?" (5:13). The reply changed that point of reference to God—"Neither . . . but as commander of the army of the LORD I have now come" (5:14). God doesn't choose sides with us. Rather, he leaves us with a question: Will we side with him?

Too many church disputes lead to members taking sides, acting like the church belongs to them. They spiritualize their actions by claiming that God is on their side. Everyone involved in such squabbling needs a strong reminder that the church belongs to God. He is at the center and should be given complete control.

The answer this man gave to Joshua provides the keys to releasing God's power in the life of a leader.

KEY NUMBER ONE: KNOW YOUR ROLE

The man identified himself as "commander of the army of the LORD" (5:14). Joshua must have been surprised that the man's job description was so similar, if not identical, to the role he envisioned for himself.

This conversation, coming as it did before the first military conflict, was an opportunity for role clarification. To be successful in any God-honoring objective, leaders must know the role God is calling them to play. And roles must not be confused with titles. For over twenty years, my title has been senior pastor, and over that time, my role has been adjusted frequently:

- Filler of the big shoes left behind by the founding pastor (1981)
- Builder of facilities (1983)
- Communicator of vision to increasing numbers of people joining us for a variety of reasons (1983 and following)
- Manager of staff (1984 and following)
- Leader of staff (1990 and following)
- Mentor to younger leaders (2000 and following)

Making role adjustments can take time. A leader may need the counsel of trusted colleagues even to see that it's time for role refocusing to take place. Our January 2000 board retreat was just such a time for me. Our board lovingly and courageously identified the roles that needed to be filled in order to move forward in our God-given mission. As much as possible, they set aside their personal feelings about the people who currently filled those in order to objectively define role requirements.

They began with the role of the senior pastor. The person currently filling that role was me. I'd love to tell you that I was completely nondefensive during the process. In reality, I vacillated between commitment to role refocusing, which I knew was necessary, and preoccupation with my desires. The board asked (again, the power of the right questions), "In light of our mission and vision, what do we need from the senior pastor of Kentwood Community Church?" They listed several abilities that were needed and some characteristics to be avoided:

Needed

- Leadership of platform ministry, exhibiting the spirit and truth of true worship.
- Vision clarification and communication. The vision must become specific and strategic so that it can be implemented and measured.
- Leadership development, including both key staff and lay individuals to fulfill the point-person roles in every area of vision pursuit.

To Be Avoided

- Personally providing necessary pastoral care and counseling for a large percentage of the congregation. The goal is to be an equipper of caregivers rather than a doer of care ministry with a few exceptions.
- Micromanaging personnel and programming. People are to be empowered to lead, and while vision alignment is critical, there must be freedom to pursue the vision in a style that fits each leader.

Having objectively defined the role of the senior pastor, the board then asked a set of questions I found intimidating. They asked:

- Do Wayne Schmidt's strengths correspond with the abilities that we need?
- Does he have the potential to develop any skill sets that he is presently lacking?
- Can he discipline himself to avoid the things that would distract him from his role?

Then I had to examine myself. I asked:

- Is the role described here one to which God is calling me?
- Am I motivated to acquire the new skills that this changed role requires?
- Should I seek a role elsewhere that better fits my God-given passions and abilities?

After prayer and discussion, both the board and I discerned that God was leading me to grow into the role as presently described.

Part of what motivated me to submit to the process was two pastoral train wrecks in nearby churches. Each of the pastors had served his congregation well for many years. Each congregation had grown from fewer than two hundred to more than five hundred people in weekly attendance, so it wasn't a matter of getting stuck at the infamous two hundred barrier. Each pastor, however, led his church by being an omnipresent caregiver and participant in every ministry committee. As gifted as they were (they sustained this pace much longer than most pastors could have), they reached their inevitable limits. They could no longer meet every need or personally guide every decision. Nor could they adjust, even though their boards repeatedly sought to assist them, to the role requirements of a senior pastor in congregations of the current size and situation. Their inability to refocus their roles resulted in several years of frustrated service, which culminated in forced resignations. That was painful for all involved because these men were deeply loved yet unwilling or unable to adjust to the changed requirements of their pastoral roles.

Their experiences forged a conviction within me that I must rise to the challenge of role refocusing—or resign. I'd had the privilege of serving Kentwood Community Church for more than two decades in a relationship that God had made beneficial for both the church and me. I resolved that I would not subtly sabotage needed changes just to preserve my place on the organizational chart. To do so would result in diminished fruitfulness, or even worse, division within the church. It might be necessary for God to provide some slow-motion time for me to understand and adjust. But I would grow, or I would go.

Of course, role refocusing would be easier if pastors filled only one role. We don't. In my life, I juggled the roles of disciple, husband, father, friend, pastor, and several others. Within my role as pastor, I juggled the roles of worship leader, vision communicator, and leadership developer. It may be that only one of those roles needs to be refocused, or perhaps all of them do.

The more permanent a role is, the more difficult it is to refocus. Most of us can adjust to new roles when we know they are temporary. For instance, I serve on several leadership teams, and on each of those teams, I fill a different role. Those roles have fewer expectations; they last only for limited time, and they're less central to my call to ministry. That makes them much easier to adjust or even resign.

What is the key to making successful role adjustments? In my life, it has been resisting the temptation to pursue self-interest in order to be a servant leader. Jesus' disciples once scrambled for the roles they thought were ideal for themselves. He challenged them with these words: "If you want to be the greatest, you must be the servant of all" (Mark 10:43 paraphrase). As followers of Christ, we are instructed, "Each of you should look not only to your own interests, but also to the interests of others" (Phil. 2:4). Paul goes on to describe how Jesus led others by providing the ultimate example of servant leadership—he sacrificed his life. A movement of God always requires servant leaders.

We were determined to promote and preserve a culture of servant leadership at Kentwood Community Church. When we saw evidence of that, we celebrated it. When we saw preoccupation with self-interest, we confronted it. We realized that if we didn't deal with it, God might send an angel with a drawn sword to help us get it right.

KEY NUMBER TWO: KNOW YOUR RESOURCES

"Are you for us or our enemies?" Joshua asked (Josh. 5:13). But the question was too limiting. It confined all impending battles to involvement by two earthly armies. The man's answer—that he belongs to neither earthly army but to the "army of the LORD" (5:14)—was a reminder of the reality of spiritual warfare.

A movement of God always involves two armies: the human and the divine. A movement of God always invites the opposition of two enemies: the human and the demonic. So, forward movement always requires spiritual leaders to faithfully fulfill their roles and humbly pray for God's resources.

Joshua's encounter with this man must have prompted a forty-year flashback. Moses had commanded Joshua to go out with some of the men of Israel to fight the Amalekites (Ex. 17:8–15). Moses stood atop a nearby hill with the staff of God in his hands. This staff had been the instrument that brought God's plagues upon Egypt, winning the release of the Hebrew people from Egypt. As long as Moses held up the staff, the Israelites dominated. But as Moses tired and lowered his hands, the tide turned against them. Finally, Moses sat down on a stone while Aaron and Hur supported his hands, holding the staff high. Joshua defeated the Amalekites in battle because the God of Israel defeated the Amalekites with the staff. Moses commemorated this powerful partnership with an altar called "The LORD is my Banner" (Ex. 17:15). Moses recognized that the necessary resources were released into hands that were lifted to the throne of the Lord.

Periodically, we need to be reminded that "our struggle is not against flesh and blood, but against the rulers, against the authorities, against the powers of this dark world and against the spiritual forces of evil in the heavenly realms" (Eph. 6:12). We're to be alert and keep on praying, regularly lifting our hands to the throne of the Lord for the resources needed for victory.

When I need a reminder of God's provision, my flashback doesn't go back forty years, and the event I recall does not result in the construction of an altar. It was during 1983, when one of my roles as senior pastor was to help with the construction of our first facility. It was a hot and humid summer Saturday afternoon. I was hammering nails while mentally rehearsing the next day's sermon. There were supposed to have been many volunteers that day, but nobody showed up. Tired, alone, and overwhelmed, I was the perfect candidate for discouragement.

Finally, I slumped in the corner of the room. Salty tears streamed down my sweaty face, which mixed with sawdust as I wiped them away. I was having an Elijah-style pity party—I was the only one left to do God's work. At that moment, my dad walked in, and I launched into a tale of woe about how the whole church was being carried on my shoulders. At that moment, my heavenly Father spoke through my earthly father. He said, "It's not your church; it's God's church. And it won't be built in your strength, but his strength. You have to do your part, but keep your hands off his part."

Ouch.

There was more. "If you keep those things straight," Dad promised, "God will never give you more than you can bear." Though I was initially resistant, I knew he was right. The burden began to lighten, and peace settled in.

Sometimes God slows us down to remind us that his purposes can only be accomplished with his power. The battle will only be won if the commander of his heavenly army shows up with sword in hand.

THE PURPOSE QUESTION

Joshua fell facedown in reverence for the commander of the Lord's army—a good response. We deal with God always from a position of submission. Then Joshua asked a second question, better framed than the first: "What message does my Lord have for his servant?" (Josh. 5:14). It was the question of purpose. Joshua was ready to take orders from the Lord.

A MOVEMENT HAS A MISSION

In 1979, I was completing undergraduate work at Marion College. During that year, a good friend entered into a prayer partnership with me. We met every Friday morning at 6:00 a.m. to seek God's mission for my life upon completion of this stage of education. I have found that God usually reveals his will first in general terms, and then gives specific focus gradually. I call this the focus funnel.

As we began to pray for clarity, I asked a series of questions:

- Am I to go on to seminary or enter ministry? The answer: ministry.
- Am I to pursue parachurch ministry or local church ministry? The answer: local church ministry.
- Am I to serve an existing church or be involved in planting a church? The answer: be involved in planting a church.
- Is there a particular place I'm to plant? The answer: southeastern Grand Rapids.

Now these answers were not audible, but I clearly sensed that there was a specific direction I should pursue unless God closed the doors. So, when the leader of our denomination for West Michigan visited the campus, I shared my sense of God's leading with him. That leader, Vaughn Drummonds, responded by laughing out loud.

He was laughing because the previous week, completely unknown to me, he had sat in the living room of Dick Wynn in Kentwood, a southeastern suburb of Grand Rapids, where Dick said, "If you find the right young man to work with me, I will serve as part-time senior pastor to plant a church in Kentwood." As mentioned earlier, Dick, who served full-time with Youth for Christ, had counseled me as I clarified my initial call to ministry. God was clearly leading us to work together.

He would continue serving Youth for Christ and give part-time leadership as I became a full-time assistant pastor.

Sensing God's mission was not a one-time event. I aim to begin each day on my knees, asking that God's calling will be accomplished in my life in the next twenty-four hours. I want to live that day in the place where his power and purpose intersect. In a facedown posture of submission, I list the top priorities in my life. First among them is this: to experience increasing intimacy with God in tandem with greater clarity, intensity, and tenacity in pursuing his calling upon my life.

The latter half of my first priority focuses on God's mission for my life.

Clarity. I lift before God each of the three roles that are my present responsibility as senior pastor. I ask God to reveal what is in line with his purpose and remove from me what is not.

Intensity. I ask God's Spirit to fill me with energy and passion for that day's pursuits. I express my longing to keep in step with his Spirit so that my energy won't be squandered on low priorities but focused on what matters.

Tenacity. I seek God's power to persevere, knowing that this will both develop my character and sustain my contribution to his mission.

When I slow down enough to begin the day this way, God's mission is clear in my mind and my motivation is strong. When I rush to begin my day and omit this time, the sense of his presence is more distant and my sense of his purpose less well-defined.

The slower motion days of 2001 allowed the leaders of Kentwood Community Church to reexamine our mission and see God's calling more clearly. I know that there are at least a hundred definitions for *mission* and *vision*, and ceaseless arguments over which is correct. At Kentwood Community Church, we chose the definitions that worked best for us: *mission*—what we must do to fulfill God's purpose for us; *vision*—what we will see as God's purpose is fulfilled through us.

Adopting those definitions led us to create a mission statement that is brief and easily communicated, and a vision statement that is longer and more detailed.

OUR MISSION

The mission of Kentwood Community Church is to obey Christ by reaching out to spiritually lost people and raising up fully committed believers who love God completely and others unconditionally.

Our mission was unashamedly Christ-centered in a culture where the name god can be attached to nearly anything yet the name of Christ is considered divisive. Our mission was lived out in obedience to Jesus Christ. It involved reaching out to spiritually lost people (the Great Commission—Matt. 28:18–20) and raising up fully committed believers who love God completely and others unconditionally (the Great Commandment—Mark 12:30–31). Our mission was simple enough to be reduced to a motto or even a logo: Reaching Out and Raising Up or R & R. When our mission functioned at its fullest, it fed on itself; we reached out to people, raised them up as fully committed believers who in turn reached out to others, who were in turn raised up. The cycle went on.

Our vision statement was more complex. It identified the attitudes and actions we would observe as we incarnated the mission in believers who belong to Kentwood Community Church. Here's an excerpt, taken from our vision for serving:

> We dream of every believer serving as part of the body of Christ and under the lordship of Christ. Where we serve is shaped by our passions; what we do utilizes our spiritual gifts; and how we serve is influenced by our personal style. More than volunteers who give of something that belongs to us, we are ministers who serve recognizing all we are and have belongs to God. We dream of every believer exercising stewardship of their time, talents, and money, permitting an uninterrupted flow of resources from God through believers to benefit his kingdom.

Joshua's reverent submission to the commander of the Lord's army evinced his willingness to join God's mission rather than a desire to coax God to adopt his plans. Joshua's attitude manifested the insight captured so powerfully by Henry Blackaby in the book *Experiencing God*.[2] Blackaby said that we are to discover what God is doing and join him where he is already at work. We're not to twist God's arm, seeking his blessing on what we've already decided to do. A movement of God always follows the mission of God.

A MOVEMENT HAS A MESSAGE

As Joshua fell facedown in reverence, he asked the man "What message does my Lord have for his servant?" (Josh. 5:14). Reverence brings receptivity to revelation. Joshua was ready to listen with the heart of a servant. He understood that a true encounter with God must be two-way, involving both asking and listening.

When our church board reached a defining moment, we often paused to engage in listening prayer. We quieted our hearts and asked God to communicate a response to some specific question. First, we clearly defined the question, and then we asked God to remove from our minds any preconceived assumptions and protect us from being swayed by human opinions or, worse yet, suggestions from our Enemy. Finally, we asked that we would hear his voice. Then we sat in silence. We jotted down thoughts that occurred to us during prayer—whether single words, paragraphs, or bits of song or Scripture. In a sense, we were brainstorming through prayer.

After praying, we asked each person to share what he or she sensed from the Lord. We looked for themes, trying to identify the concepts that resonated most fully with the group. We took these thoughts into consideration as we formed a final decision.

We didn't leave the room and announce to the world, "God told us to . . ." Yet we left those meetings knowing that quieting our hearts before God, listening carefully for his leading, and testing what we'd heard in the context of community raised the likelihood that we would choose the direction God intended for us.

As Joshua listened, the commander replied, "Take off your sandals, for the place where you are standing is holy" (Josh. 5:15). Moses received this same message before his mission to Egypt. Now, it was given to Joshua before he embarked on his mission in the Promised Land. Joshua responded with obedience.

Not surprisingly, Joshua understood the message the first time God delivered it. A drawn sword is a powerful communication tool. Yet for me, more often than not, it takes repeated revelation for God to get through. I'm more like Samuel who needed to hear the call of God three times before he realized what it was (1 Sam. 3). I am often moving too fast or am too preoccupied to develop the ears to hear and eyes to see God's revelation.

I am humbled by the fact that God graciously repeats his messages so I can be included in what he is doing. It's painful for me, after finally receiving God's message, to look back over months or even years and see the times God tried to communicate with me, but I didn't hear. Hindsight has shown me the need to regularly ask God to make his will plain—and help me get it the first time.

For me, that happens only when I experience a Spirit-generated combination of humility and purity. Without that, I'd never have the tenacity to persevere in my calling. At times, I've begged to be released from the responsibilities God has placed upon my shoulders. Rather than giving that release, God has nearly always used those occasions to imprint this truth upon my heart: Obedience requires perseverance.

The encounter with God's messenger changed Joshua's life and his leadership. And it's no wonder. When God's power and purpose come together, it's time to take off our sandals. Something holy is about to happen.

12

OVERCOMING OBSTACLES

Joshua 6

Momentum Builder	**Momentum Buster**
Momentum is developed by exercising your will and strategizing solutions.	Momentum is drained by failing to build upon God-given victories.

People seek God's will in many different ways. Among the most common is the open-door-closed-door approach. That's when we pray, "If it is your will Lord, open the door and give me the courage to walk through it. If it is not your will, close the door so tight that I can't pry it open."

But what if the objective is God's will, yet the door is shut tight? That's exactly the position in which Joshua found himself. God had personally revealed to Joshua that it was his will to give the Promised Land to Israel. Yet the first city they were to conquer, Jericho, "was

> "The harder the conflict, the more glorious the triumph.
> What we obtain too cheaply, we esteem too lightly."
>
> —THOMAS PAINE

tightly shut up because of the Israelites. No one went out and no one came in" (6:1).

> "A great door for effective work has opened to me,
> and there are many who oppose me."
>
> —1 CORINTHIANS 16:9

Spiritual leaders understand that even when a project is God's will, there may be obstacles to overcome. Even when we're certain of God's purpose and working in his power, we may bump our noses on some closed doors. There are always barriers to victory. These barriers remind us that there are some openings only God can create. They may slow us down a bit as we work and pray to overcome or go around them, but we should not be intimidated by these obstacles or ignore them.

ANALYZING OBSTACLES

One way to get a handle on obstacles is to develop an annual personal ministry action plan (MAP). The MAP is developed in three parts:

M—Momentum goals. These are the areas having the greatest potential for fruitfulness in the coming year. This should be a short list, focused on investment in the areas where the most momentum can be generated.

A—Activities. These are areas of practical faithfulness. They are core ingredients of the position that the staff member or lay minister fills. Completing them doesn't create momentum, but neglecting them would lead to a loss of momentum.

P—Possibilities. These are areas worth exploring but dependent upon factors or people beyond our control.

For each momentum goal, create a force field analysis with two columns. In the left column, identify supporting forces—resources that can be leveraged to achieve the goal. In the right column, list opposing forces—sources of resistance to achieving the goal.

FORCE FIELD ANALYSIS

Supporting   Opposing

Thorough analysis always reveals that both forces are present. The existence of opposing forces does not indicate the absence of God's will. Rather, it shows where additional prayer, perseverance, and planning may be required.

I'll never forget a conversation I had with a pastor one day in my office. He knew it was God's will for his church to relocate. Ideal property had been purchased, and he had the credibility to lead the transition. He went on to share that he had one board member who was a little hesitant and that 10 percent of his congregation was fairly resistant to the change. His decision was to pray that there would be complete unanimity of the board and congregation as an indication that it was God's will to relocate. That unanimity never materialized, and 90 percent of the congregation, as well as the progress of the church, were held captive by a hesitant or resistant few. Discontentment grew, the pastor left, and a new pastor was called, who led the congregation to relocate. Had the church become completely unified around the relocation? No. The new pastor did a force field analysis, rightly determined that the supportive forces exceeded the opposing forces, and led them forward. A few members left, but many more people have been reached for Christ.

Making the decision to move forward, however, is not merely a matter of adding up the numbers. There's another factor in the equation.

Let's imagine Joshua sitting down on a rock and developing a force field analysis.

SUPPORTING FORCES	OPPOSING FORCES
God's promise of deliverance (6:2)	City tightly shut up (6:1)
Willing spiritual leaders (6:6)	Opposing king and fighting men (6:2)
United people (6:7)	Troops with no previous battle experience

His list appears to be balanced—the number of supporting forces equals the number of opposing forces. So, what made the difference for Joshua that gave him the confidence to move ahead? "Then the LORD said to Joshua . . ." (6:2). He heard what God had to say.

God's voice tips the scale in any spiritual decision. Joshua had initiated this movement into the Promised Land in response to the voice of God. God had repeatedly instructed Joshua to "be strong and courageous" (1:6–9) in conquering the land. Now, Joshua had, once again, personally communicated with God. Responding to God's personal promise was the key not only to initiating this movement, but also to continuing it. God didn't stop speaking to Joshua, and Joshua didn't stop listening.

DEFINING STRATEGIES

God spoke to Joshua before anyone else. That's the way God often works with leaders. He reveals his goals and the steps to take in reaching them to the leader first. That leader gets the message earlier and clearer than the rest of the people. This is both God's gift to the leader and the burden a leader must bear.

SEEING THE GOD-GIVEN GOAL

I've often heard spiritual leaders say something like, "It's so clear to me; why can't anybody else see it?" One reason is that the leader usually has a vantage point to see the whole picture while others see only their part in the picture. That leader can look over the forest, while others can't see the forest for the trees because they are so deeply involved in one area of ministry. Another reason is that leaders see both the possibilities and the problems while others may be either overwhelmed by the problems or enamored with the possibilities and be unable to realistically imagine the outcome. The capacity to sense the vision earlier and clearer than others contributes to the loneliness of a leader.

By God's design, the leader is granted the privilege of seeing things others are yet to see and seeing them with greater clarity. God empowers leaders to see what others don't and then commissions those leaders to help others see and act upon the vision.

What did this supernatural seeing reveal to Joshua? "See, I have delivered Jericho into your hands, along with its king and its fighting men" (6:2). What would Joshua have seen physically at this point? A walled city filled with fighting men, commanded by a king. Nothing but opposition. What did he see supernaturally? He saw God delivering the city, its king, and its fighting men into Israel's hands. Leaders see what others don't. Where others see obstacles and opposition, God reveals opportunity.

The question for Joshua, and for any spiritual leader, is which vision to trust: the physical or the spiritual. Do we have spiritual eyes to see and ears to hear what God is saying to us? For Joshua, this was not a matter of fabricating a goal to pursue and framing it in the words, "God told me." This was God's promise, which he had given before, that he would give victory. The Bible often describes God as a deliverer. Sometimes God delivers us from things, while at other times he delivers things to us. In this case, the God-given goal was the deliverance of Jericho into the hands of his people as a first step in a long-term plan to conquer the Promised Land.

When Joshua personally heard from God, he understood his role as a spiritual leader. Spiritual leadership is not a matter of conquering territory. It is a matter of positioning God's people to receive what God has promised to them. The leader must help God's people both to see God's goal and to act in God's power to reach it.

DEFINING THE STRATEGY FOR VICTORY

Joshua had been given his mission. The specific steps to accomplishing that mission had been specified in a clear vision. The first of those steps had been crystallized into an immediate goal. To see and communicate the mission, vision, and goal is the responsibility of every spiritual leader charged with managing a movement of God. And there is one more element required for success: A strategy for reaching each goal must be identified.

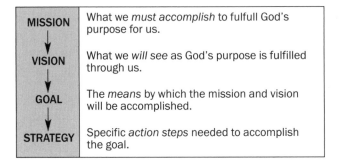

MISSION	What we *must accomplish* to fulfull God's purpose for us.
VISION	What we *will see* as God's purpose is fulfilled through us.
GOAL	The *means* by which the mission and vision will be accomplished.
STRATEGY	Specific *action steps* needed to accomplish the goal.

The strategy was the last element of the plan revealed to Joshua. And an unusual strategy it was. Here are the action steps that God indicated:

March around the city once with all the armed men. Do this for six days. Have the seven priests carry trumpets of rams' horns in front of the ark. On the seventh day, march around the city seven times, with the priests blowing the trumpets. When you hear them sound a long blast on the trumpets, have all the people give a loud shout; then the wall of the city will collapse and the people will go up, every man straight in. (Josh. 6:3–5)

What kind of strategy is this? The Israelites must have wondered whether it was the product of inspiration or insanity. It was certainly a strategy that had never been used before, nor would be again. It was a faith-based plan that involved a series of actions that were tailor-made to reach the goal in a way that could bring glory only to God. When spiritual strategies are used, the goal is reached and God is revered.

The more one progresses in the development of a God-given calling, the more unique it becomes. The mission of Kentwood Community Church was based on the Great Commission (Matt. 28:18–20) and the Great Commandment (Mark 12:30–31). The key components—reaching out and raising up—are biblically sound and could be generally applied to thousands of churches. Our vision, however, reflected our situation more specifically. Our goals were unique, probably applicable only to this congregation. Our strategies, therefore, were highly individualized. That's the way it must be with any congregation. Strategies are highly specialized because the steps a church takes to reach its goals will be shaped by the answers to these personalized questions:

- What are the goals that God is leading us to accomplish?
- What resources are available to us?
- What is unique about our history and culture that will affect the way our actions are perceived and received?
- What is unique about our ministry context?
- Do our proposed action steps align with our church's values and beliefs?

In answering these questions, the highest compliment any leader can receive is the one extended to the "men of Issachar, who understood the times and knew what Israel should do" (1 Chron. 12:32). A spiritual leader must understand the uniqueness of his or her situation and then determine which steps should be taken to reach the God-given goal.

One of Kentwood Community Church's two key objectives was to reach out to the community. Outreach can be accomplished through a variety of strategies. The strategy we used may be illustrated by an outstretched hand, with each finger representing one dimension of the plan.

KENTWOOD COMMUNITY CHURCH OUTREACH STRATEGY	
Thumb	Sensitivity to people and promptings of God's Spirit
First Finger	Prayer for spiritually lost people
Second Finger	Evangelistic style that is most natural to you
Third Finger	Presentation of the gospel
Fourth Finger	Invitation to an event of appropriate evangelistic intensity

Thumb. The thumb reminds us to increase our awareness of divine moments of opportunity by raising our sensitivity to God and others. Why do some Christians go months or years without having an opportunity to share the gospel while others regularly see opportune moments? Opportunities come as we are in tune to the Spirit and dialed-in to the needs of others. Intentionally raising our awareness in these two areas empowers us to see and seize more opportunities.

First Finger. The first finger represents intentional and regular prayer for people who are spiritually lost. We called this our Four Heaven's Sake list. We encouraged everyone in our congregation to keep such a list, identifying at least four people for whom they will regularly pray.

Second Finger. The second finger represents our evangelistic style. The Becoming a Contagious Christian course has helped many people identify their style of sharing the gospel. Some are intellectual, confrontational, invitational, or some other style in their approach. There are a number of ways to approach evangelism. When people work within their style, they are more likely to be effective.

Third Finger. The third finger is a reminder that we must know a simple way to present the gospel. If a believer can verbally explain or draw on a dinner napkin the simple steps to entering a personal relationship with Jesus Christ, he or she will be prepared to offer an invitation when the time comes.

Fourth Finger. The fourth finger represents invitation. We encouraged members to invite spiritually lost friends to events that had an evangelistic intensity appropriate for their spiritual journey. We developed a scale of one to five to communicate the evangelistic intensity of our ministries. A one event was low intensity, a fun event without prayer or preaching. A five event was a high intensity event at which we made a compelling presentation of the options of eternal life in heaven or hell, and then offered an invitation and awaited a response. It was up to members to discern which level of intensity would help their friends to take the next step.

Our strategy for outreach reflected our unique situation and helped us to clearly see what we needed to do in order to equip others to participate in the mission of reaching out.

IMPLEMENTING THE STRATEGY EFFECTIVELY

God's strategy for Joshua doesn't mean that we, too, should organize a march. The strategy was unique to the situation. But there are characteristics of this strategy that can be applied to any movement of the people of God.

LEADERSHIP CROSS-SECTION

First, it was communicated to and elicited commitment from a cross-section of leaders. The first group Joshua called for were the priests (Josh. 6:6–7). These spiritual leaders had fresh faith because of the miraculous leadership they had recently provided in crossing the Jordan (3:14—4:18). Joshua also involved the armed guard (6:7, 9) who would serve as a wall of protection around the priests and the ark of the covenant. This march would involve the participation of all leaders in ways that were consistent with their roles.

Implementation of a sound strategy begins with the identification of influential people within the church. This identification is not an act of favoritism but recognizes that there are opinion leaders in every organization who are crucial to a strategy's success. For instance, the Pareto Principle, also known as the 80/20 Rule, holds that 80 percent of our results come from 20 percent of our actions.[1] Many churches have found that—

- 80 percent of the income is given by 20 percent of the people.
- 80 percent of the serving is done by 20 percent of the people.
- 80 percent of the prayer is offered by 20 percent of the people.
- 80 percent of the witnessing is accomplished by 20 percent of the people.

So a leader in a church of two hundred people might ask, "Who are the forty people (20 percent) who are most influential in the life of our church?"

Having identified the opinion leaders, there are two questions to consider. First, what is the best way to communicate with them about the steps that are planned: one-on-one, in small groups, by phone, in writing? Second, what type of involvement will be needed from them: prayer, feedback, specific responsibility for implementing some part of the strategy? When opinion leaders have a connection with the leader of the movement, they take ownership of the initiative.

SYMBOLS

Second, Joshua's God-given strategy was filled with symbols that had significance to the people. The centerpiece of their movement was the ark of the covenant (6:6). This most sacred piece of tabernacle furniture was approximately five feet long, three feet wide, and three feet deep. It signified the Lord's throne and had been the focal point in their movement across the Jordan River (3:3).

The priests were instructed to carry trumpets. These instruments, fashioned from rams' horns, were not musical instruments but were used for signaling in religious and military contexts. Their sound announced the presence of the Lord (see 2 Sam. 6:15; 1 Chron. 15:28; Zech. 9:14).

The number seven was also used symbolically. Seven priests were to carry trumpets (Josh. 6:6) and march around the city on seven consecutive days, marching seven times around on the seventh day (6:15). This called to mind the seven days of creation and the significance of the number seven as a symbol of completion or perfection.

A sound strategy makes use of symbols that are significant to the people. For instance, Kentwood Community Church's vision included stewardship: "More than volunteers who give of something that belongs to us, we are ministers who serve recognizing all that we are and have belongs to God. We dream of every believer exercising stewardship of their time, talents, and money, permitting an uninterrupted flow of resources from God through believers to benefit his kingdom." So, when I taught on financial freedom through biblical stewardship, I used ten large, colored, interchangeable blocks as symbols. Each block represented one tenth of a person's income.

Gold	Green	Blue	Blue	Red
Blue	Blue	Blue	Blue	Red

Gold Block. This 10 percent represents the tithe.

Green Block. This 10 percent represents savings.

Blue Blocks. These blocks represent spending.

Red Blocks. These blocks represent debt.

I arranged the blocks in different patterns to represent different financial situations in which people found themselves. Since I taught on this subject several times, whenever people saw the blocks on the platform, they thought of the phrase, "God's pattern for financial freedom." The blocks became a significant symbol to our maturing stewards.

BROAD-BASED PARTICIPATION

Third, Joshua's strategy was implemented through broad-based participation by the people. While there were specialized roles for the leaders, every man had an opportunity to march. Their participation in the march represented their confidence in the strategy that had been revealed to Joshua. It also allowed them to share in the victory that was to be celebrated when the walls of Jericho came down. Later on, when the walls did fall, "everyone charged straight in" (6:20) and joined in devoting the city to the Lord.

God gave the people easy first steps for involvement: "Go for a walk" (6:7) ". . . keep quiet" (6:10) ". . . then shout" (6:16). These steps also developed obedience and perseverance in the people. While the leaders had more complex responsibilities in keeping with their roles, the followers were included. They were given a part that included them without overwhelming them.

A sound strategy identifies easy first steps that allow for broad participation. For instance, when starting another worship service, identify people who will pray for it, serve as ushers, greeters, hosts, or in other roles. Be creative in identifying as many simple roles as possible to provide significant ownership by the greatest number of people.

THE GOD MOMENT

Joshua's strategy identified the critical God moment in the process. After circling Jericho for the seventh time on the seventh day, the priests were to blow their trumpets and all the people were to shout, "For the LORD has given you the city" (6:16). At this point, every person in the march was undoubtedly praying that God would show up. God always does things in a way that makes it clear that he is responsible and that he alone should receive the glory. The Israelites had done their part; now it was time for God to do his part. This is not to say that God was less present in any other step of the strategy, but that the table was set for God to bring victory in a miraculous way—a way that only he could.

A sound strategy will identify the God moment. In a service, it might be the open altar time. In a celebration, it might be the time when praise is given for what has been accomplished. In a fundraising campaign, it might be the moment people are asked to register their prayer-based financial commitment. The God moment in any strategy must be the focus of fervent prayer as leaders and people ask God to reveal himself in such a way that all who are spiritually sensitive will conclude that God did something great.

GIVING GLORY TO GOD

The successful victory brought about by this strategy resulted in the city of Jericho being "devoted to the LORD" (6:17). That process of devotion is unique to the Old Testament, a reflection of the Israelites' system of sacrificial worship. However, what they did physically after their victory is precisely what we should do spiritually, devoting ourselves completely to the Lord. That involves four specific actions that I call the motion of devotion.

ELIMINATION

Devotion involves the elimination of all that is contrary to God. "They devoted the city to the LORD and destroyed with the sword every living thing in it—men and women, young and old, cattle, sheep and donkeys" (6:21). Moses, Joshua's predecessor and mentor, had ordered the Israelites not to leave anything alive that breathed, or those survivors might teach the Israelites to sin and to worship other gods (Deut. 20:16–20). Eliminating them would keep the Israelites from idolatry and its accompanying moral corruption.

Today, being fully devoted to God involves removing from our lives anything that leads toward idolatry. Idols are God's competitors in our lives, those things that vie for the first place that belongs only to him. Conquering requires cleansing.

PRESERVATION

Devotion also involves preserving that which is valuable to God. Upon entering Jericho, the Israelites were to keep away from the devoted things, for taking them would bring about one's destruction and the possibility of wider judgment on the camp of Israel. Everything made of silver, gold, bronze, or iron was to be considered sacred and was to be given to the Lord's treasury (Josh. 6:18–19). These metals would be used in the creation of sacred objects and places. What was won in warfare would be woven into worship.

While it's vital that we remove from our lives what is contrary to God, it is equally important that we preserve what he values. This preservation often involves the transformation of things that were once used for earthly purposes so that they may be used for eternal purposes. That phrase "the Lord's treasury" reminds me of a conversation that Jesus had with his followers one day. He wanted them to understand that there are two treasuries. One is earthly; it can be lost and is of little lasting value. The other is heavenly; it can't be lost and has eternal value. Jesus concluded his teaching by saying, "For where your treasure is, there your heart will be also" (Matt. 6:21).

COMPLETION

Completion is another aspect of devotion. Devotion involves the completion of all promises we have made to God and others. When Jericho fell, Joshua honored the promise that had been made to Rahab (Josh. 6:25). As mentioned earlier, when Joshua sent spies into the land, they met with Rahab, who recognized that "the LORD your God is God in heaven above and on the earth below" (2:11). When the spies were threatened with capture, they promised that if she would help them escape, all who were in her house would be spared in the coming battle. Rahab was to leave a scarlet cord tied in her window until the Israelites returned, which she did. She and her family were spared and lived among the Israelites as they continued to conquer the land.

Joshua kept his promise and showed that he served a God who keeps his word. It also made clear that the destruction of those living in the land was not undertaken because the Israelites were in some way superior to their enemies. Rather, it was based on the refusal by those enemies to honor God. Rahab was saved because she submitted herself to God's will and participated in it. She placed her faith in God, and she—along with her household—demonstrated that faith by seeking sanctuary in her house as the spies had instructed.

Our personal devotion to God is demonstrated when we honor God's promise of salvation by offering the good news to others. For God does "not [want] anyone to perish, but everyone to come to repentance" (2 Pet. 3:9).

REPUTATION

Finally, devotion involves building God's reputation for his glory not our own. After the victory, Joshua pronounced a solemn oath that focused all attention squarely upon God (Josh. 6:26). In so doing, he used the day's gain as leverage for lasting commitment.

"So the LORD was with Joshua, and his fame spread throughout the land" (6:27). God's victory gave Joshua added credibility with the Israelites, strengthening his leadership credentials for future battle. Leaders must constantly reinvest in the mission, just as a financial investor automatically reinvests a client's dividends to keep his account growing. Leaders are stewards of fame, or credibility, and must invest it well. What is the best reason for being famous? Because it's evident that God is with you. A good reputation is a resource that can be used to create movement in the future.

Success can sometimes bring leaders financial rewards, recognition, speaking engagements, and writing opportunities—none of which are wrong in and of themselves. But if those rewards become our focus, we'll soon find ourselves playing it safe in order to preserve the perks. Leaders must constantly reinvest their time, energy, and attention to invigorate the forward movement of God's kingdom.

On this point, my accountability partnership has been a great benefit. Each opportunity I receive to travel, speak, or write is screened by my accountability partner before acceptance. First of all, I need to be living a balanced personal life and be consistently reaching my accountability goals. Second, I need to faithfully fulfill the leadership role to which God has called me. To determine how I'm doing, I use questions based on the motion of devotion:

- Have I consistently eliminated from my life attitudes or actions that are not pleasing to God?
- How well have I preserved the values and priorities that are most precious to God?
- Have I kept the promises I've made so I do not neglect present commitments in my haste to make new ones?

- Have I reinvested whatever ministry credibility I have gained for God's glory rather than using it for personal gain?

If these questions can be answered positively, then the opportunity is screened based on how well it fits with my life calling. That prevents me from accepting opportunities based on the glamour of the location or the size of the honorarium. Instead, I'm able to choose those opportunities that best equip others to increase their positive effect on the lives they touch.

It helps me to picture the motion of devotion as a flywheel.

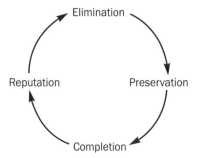

Elimination

Reputation

Preservation

Completion

A flywheel starts slowly and is hard to turn at the beginning. It requires a great deal of energy to overcome inertia and make the wheel move. But once it begins, the wheel revolves faster and faster, requiring less effort. As my life progresses, I want my acts of devotion to God to occur more readily, even automatically. For many spiritual leaders, the motion of devotion loses momentum as the years pass. God's will is that our devotion should gain momentum with every passing year.

13

THE DEBILITATING
DANGER OF DECEPTION

Joshua 7–9

Momentum Builder	**Momentum Buster**
Momentum is developed by acknowledging the truth about yourself and others.	Momentum is drained by deceiving and being deceived.

Success is dangerous. The greater the victory, the greater the danger. Our greatest victory can set us up for our greatest defeat. That's because success affects our perceptions of the world and ourselves, allowing deception to creep in. When things are happening quickly, it's even easier to be deceived. That's another reason that God sometimes slows us down: to help us see what has really happened and bring debilitating secrets to light.

Joshua and the nation of Israel were coming down from an awesome victory. This was the first time their troops had needed to trust God for

> "When our knowing exceeds our sensing, we will no longer be deceived by the illusions of our senses."
>
> —WALTER RUSSELL

victory in a military offensive. Their faith positioned them to witness a miracle. The seemingly impenetrable walls of Jericho had collapsed, and the inhabitants of the city were completely conquered. This significant city was the gateway to the Promised Land. Its defeat marked the beginning of what could only be a series of spectacular victories.

> "And this is my prayer: that your love may abound more and more in knowledge and depth of insight, so that you may be able to discern what is best and may be pure and blameless until the day of Christ."
> —PHILIPPIANS 1:9-10

Next was the city of Ai. The spies had checked it out and determined that it would offer weak resistance. It wouldn't even be worth sending all the troops (7:3). They recommended that Joshua send two thousand or three thousand troops to conquer the city while the rest relaxed. Joshua agreed, sent about three thousand men, and waited for the report of victory. The battle did not go at all as he expected. The men of Ai conquered the army of Israel. When they fled, the army of Ai chased and killed thirty-six Israelites. The anticipated victory turned into an unexpected defeat.

In Joshua 7–9, deception crept into the Israelite camp, distancing them from God and preventing them from enjoying his full blessing. Deception is a cancer. It grows inside a seemingly healthy leader. More than one movement of God has been destroyed by the self-deception of its leaders. There are two sources of deception: It can originate within a movement of God based on the presence of disobedience, or it can come from without based on the absence of discernment.

DECEPTION ON THE INSIDE:
THE PRESENCE OF DISOBEDIENCE

The battle of Jericho appeared to have been a complete victory. But that public perception masked the private reality of deception. Joshua and the other leaders did not yet know what God knew: "the Israelites acted unfaithfully in regard to the devoted things" (7:1).

ROBBING GOD

Because Jericho was the first city conquered in Canaan, it was the firstfruits of the Promised Land. A foundational principle of Scripture is that firstfruits belong to God. They are to be given to him as an act of worship. In the economy of the ancient world, income came from the land. So, God cast the command in agricultural terms: "Bring the best of the firstfruits of your soil to the house of the LORD your God" (Ex. 23:19). When Jericho was conquered, all the silver, gold, bronze, and iron were supposed to have gone into the treasury of the tabernacle. But one man, Achan, had robbed God by taking some of these devoted things for himself. Robbing God of what is rightfully his removes his blessing and replaces it with his anger.

That was true for the Israelites as a nation, and it is also true for God's people individually. Centuries after the defeat at Ai, the last book of the Old Testament recorded God's haunting question, "Will a man rob God?" The prophet Malachi carried on a rhetorical debate with God, asking, "How do we rob you?" God answered, "In tithes and offerings" (Mal. 3:8). The tithe (one-tenth), the firstfruits of their income, was to be devoted to the Lord and brought into his storehouse. God's people were keeping some of that devoted portion for themselves. As a result, they lived under a curse instead of experiencing the fulfillment of God's promise to 'throw open the floodgates of heaven and pour out so much blessing that you will not have room enough for it" (3:10).

Robbing God isn't a matter of mugging him. We don't steal from God by overpowering him and wresting some possession from his grasp. Robbing God is more like embezzling. An embezzler is someone who's been given access to another person's possessions in order to manage them. But instead of acting faithfully, an embezzler takes the person's possessions for his use. Incredibly, many embezzlers live under the deception that they somehow have a right to do this. They come to see the other person's wealth as theirs.

God owns everything, including the homes, possessions, and money that we hold in trust for him. He graciously gives us up to 90 percent of what we hold to use for saving, investing, and spending. He expects at least 10 percent of that trust to be returned to his storehouse—the local church and ministries that flow from it. This tithe is to be taken off the top—the firstfruits. When we divert that tithe from his intended purpose (giving) into our pockets (saving, investing, spending), we embezzle from him. We rob God.

In the case of Achan, the secret sin of one man dramatically affected many people and the momentum of the movement of God. I've often wondered, "Does the secret sin of embezzling God's resources by not tithing, especially if the individual is a leader, have the potential to affect a congregation's momentum?" If the answer is yes, it's no wonder many churches are impotent, for there is an epidemic of embezzling among Christians in our materialistic culture.

REVERSING MOMENTUM

Disobedience caused by deception is the quickest way to lose or reverse momentum. That's true both personally and organizationally. Achan may have convinced himself that secret sin doesn't matter—what they don't know won't hurt them. Secret sin, however, has public consequences. The God who was with Israel (Josh. 6:27) now allowed his anger to burn against them (7:1).

Disobedience by one led to the defeat of all. This defeat brought not only physical loss (death), but also emotional and spiritual loss as "the hearts of the people melted" (7:5). Earlier, when the spies were scouting the land, Rahab had described that same fear running through Israel's enemies. She said, "Our hearts melted and everyone's courage failed because of you" (2:11). What had been true of their enemies was now true of them. This was a momentum meltdown. Just as small acts of obedience build momentum, small acts of disobedience stall it. Achan's disobedience resulted in a loss of confidence that permeated the whole nation of Israel. It can happen to whole congregations too.

RECOGNIZING THE PROBLEM

Joshua, the leader, was unaware of Achan's sin. God sometimes slows things down—or even lets them grind to a halt—so leaders can become aware of issues beneath the surface. When things are moving quickly, leaders tend to hydroplane. Downshifting may be necessary in order to recognize and deal with deceptions that have taken place.

Joshua responded to the devastating situation with actions that showed deep humility. He tore his clothes, fell facedown before the ark, and remained in God's presence rather than rushing out to fix the problem (7:6). The other leaders of Israel did the same, adding to their expression of regret by sprinkling dust on their heads.

Joshua prayed, asking the question that was on everyone's mind, "Ah, Sovereign LORD, why . . . ?" (7:7–9). Simultaneously submitting to God's sovereignty and asking the why question is the key to receiving revelation. While Joshua's prayer started and ended strong, his confusion was evident. Let's trace his emotions in this prayer.

First, Joshua blamed God. His question assumed that God's leadership was the source of the problem: "Why did you ever bring this people across the Jordan to deliver us into the hands of the Amorites to destroy us?" (7:7).

Next, he lost vision and even wished the Israelites had never moved forward in the first place: "If only we had been content to stay on the other side of the Jordan!" (7:7). In this case, Joshua's feigned contentment with the previous situation was a cover for a lack of faith. In despair, he succumbed to the danger of the "if only" syndrome. His misplaced regret for crossing the Jordan was not a substitute for repentance.

Finally, he became selfish. Joshua's self-centered concern was for what he could say about the predicament (7:8) and for what the enemy would do to them (7:9). That's where many responsible people begin their prayers—with what they can say about the situation.

Joshua's honest prayer, like the prayers of many struggling spiritual leaders, focused more on himself than on God. It reflected a certain double-mindedness. Eventually, however, Joshua moved beyond self-absorption to concern for God's reputation: "What then will you do for your own great name?" (7:9). Spiritual leaders must rise above their concern for the management of a crisis. Their ultimate concern must be for the potential impact of the situation upon God's reputation.

God's answer (7:10–12) confirmed that Joshua's constructive humility (7:6) had degenerated into destructive self-pity (7:10). There are times to kneel and times to take a stand. This was a time to "stand up!" (7:10). Let's follow God's response to Joshua.

First, God revealed the area of disobedience and deception (7:11). Israel had violated the covenant God told them to keep. They had stolen from God by taking devoted things as their possessions. They had lied.

Next, God revealed the reason for their defeat: "That is why . . ." (7:12). God gave a direct answer to Joshua's earlier why question (7:7). Disobedience and deception result in defeat and destruction (7:11–12).

Finally, God distanced himself from his people, but let it be known that this distance could be overcome by deeds of repentance (7:12). Joshua's original commission had been accompanied by a promise: "As I was with Moses, so I will be with you; I will never leave you nor forsake you" (1:5). Now Joshua was reminded of the condition of this promise: obedience. "I will not be with you anymore unless you destroy whatever among you is devoted to destruction" (7:12).

This is the downward spiral of deception seen in so many leaders and churches.

Deception

Disobedience

Defeat

Distance from
God

Tragically, many leaders continue to try moving forward without the empowering presence of God. Where there is defeat, God says we need to go back to where it all began. We need to return to the root of the problem—disobedience and deception.

SEEKING GOD

To deal with deception, one must confront the truth. God forced Israel to do that after the devastating defeat at Ai. Just as God involved all the people in the victory of Jericho, so he also involved everyone in dealing with deception. The steps he led Israel through then are similar to the steps he now uses to lead his people in replacing deception with devotion.

Consecration. First, God instructed the people to consecrate themselves to him (7:13). This ritual of purification was the necessary preparation for meeting with God. When the people stood before their holy God, they had to be holy people. There would be no revelation from God until his people were first consecrated to him.

While we no longer use rituals of purification, we, too, must be consecrated to God if he is to speak to us. He wants to know that we are ready to be both "hearers and doers" of what he will communicate to us.

Presentation. Next, God set a time—the next morning—when the people would present themselves to him (7:14–18). They would present themselves to God tribe by tribe, clan by clan, family by family, man by man. God stipulated a process that would reveal the exact source of the deception. Joshua began leading them through this process early the next morning (7:16).

What would be an equivalent process for a church that wanted to discover why God was distant from them? Notice that God led his people through a process that moved from general to specific. Like peeling back the layers of an onion, he brought them to the core of the issue. A church might approximate that by conducting a self-analysis that examined department by department, ministry by ministry, class by class, group by group. How courageous it would be for a church to undertake a time of congregational soul-searching in order to discover the reasons they were not experiencing spiritual victory.

CAUSES OF DECEPTION IN CHURCHES

Congregational self-deception is a cancer that first spreads and then kills churches. In many churches, the search for new ideas and tools to create church health is a way of avoiding the problem. What are some common causes of deception?

Abuse of Power. Pastors or lay persons may become consumed with personal power. They naïvely view a my-way-or-the-highway approach to conflict resolution as evidence of strong leadership. They blindly believe that their personal agenda is God's plan for ministry. The abuser of power divides the fellowship and restricts vision yet imagines others as the cause of the problem.

Lack of Accountability. When a head-in-the-sand approach to leadership is substituted for speaking the truth in love, there are many possible deceptions. Money may be spent in ways it shouldn't be. A relationship that has become emotionally or physically inappropriate may be allowed to continue. Personal and organizational discipline may be sacrificed as promises are broken and important questions are left unasked and unanswered.

Legalism. Legalism is the introduction of new standards of spirituality that go beyond the clear teaching of Scripture. This problem is as old as Eve, who falsely quoted God as saying they weren't to touch the tree at the center of the garden. God had said only that they were not to eat from it. Legalism begets false pride in adhering to one's own criteria for spirituality—usually a list of dos and don'ts—rather than the humility that comes from obeying God's simple commands.

Lukewarmness. Lukewarmness occurs when people are blinded to their true spiritual needs and exercise a faith devoid of repentance. In lukewarm churches, the call to holiness falls on deaf ears, if it is issued at all. The church becomes nothing more than a social club.

Cynicism. Cynicism is an attitude that condemns new or different ideas without consideration. Cynics imagine themselves as defenders of tradition or discerners of true spirituality, but the hallmark of their Christianity is criticism rather than love. That critical spirit repels new people and new ideas, leaving the cynic with the smug impression that he has honored God.

CAUSES OF DECEPTION IN OURSELVES

Deception is equally cancerous in the life of a leader. We must engage in a regular and relentless process of identifying self-deception and breaking free from it. If God seems distant and spiritual defeat is prevalent, a leader should ask soul-searching questions in these areas.

Physical. Am I a good steward of my body, God's temple? Do I lack self-control so that I am driven by fleshly desires?

Mental. Are my thoughts centered on what is excellent and praiseworthy? Are my attitudes like those of Christ Jesus in every area of my life?

Emotional. Do my feelings follow my faith or lead it? Are my emotions appropriately expressed to God and others?

Financial. Do I rob God? Am I in bondage to debt or addicted to spending? Do I find security in my savings and investments rather than in God?

Relational. Do I speak the truth in love? Is there an unresolved conflict or root of bitterness in my life?

Spiritual. Do I quiet my heart daily to experience intimacy with God? Do I respond to the Spirit's prompting in my life?

I make it a daily practice to parade each area of my life before God in prayer so he can specifically reveal any self-deception.

Yet I can easily fool myself. I must never assume that I will automatically see my weaknesses. That's the nature of self-deception, after all. The apostle Paul had a healthy suspicion of his conscience: "My conscience is clear, but that does not make me innocent. It is the Lord who judges me" (1 Cor. 4:4).

Frankly, I don't always trust myself to answer these self-accountability questions honestly. So I periodically have others examine my life, namely my spouse, my accountability partner, staff members, and church board members. I've seen many colleagues fail morally at times when they perceived themselves to be spiritually strong. I've heard leaders I love excuse ongoing sins of gluttony, greed, anger, and selfishness. When they continue to live with self-deception, the power of their personal example dies a slow death.

REMOVING SELF-DECEPTION

Self-deception by either a church or leader is debilitating, but it need not be fatal. Once deception has been identified, it can be dealt with. Here are the steps that God used in moving Israel out of self-deception into the power of truth.

Confession. When all the people had presented themselves, the searchlight fell upon Achan (7:19–23). Interestingly, Joshua didn't respond with anger but addressed Achan in a fatherly fashion—"My son" (7:19). He encouraged Achan to glorify God by revealing what he had done. God receives praise when that which is hidden comes to light. Achan's confession ("It is true!") in verses 20–21, included a statement of both his sinful action ("This is what I have done") and the attitude that fueled it ("I coveted").

Most Christians probably think of making music as the primary way in which they praise God. Many of our musical offerings, in fact, are labeled praise songs. But shouldn't we also offer the praise of confession to God? God is glorified when disobedience is acknowledged and fresh surrender is made to him.

Devotion. After Achan confessed, that which was supposed to be devoted to the Lord was finally given to him (7:24–26). Tragically, the consequences of Achan's secret sin had a very public impact on those he loved. His deception cost not only his life, but also the lives of his family members as well as thirty-six soldiers (7:5). The Lord brought disaster on the one who brought disaster upon his people.

Later repentance never substitutes for earlier obedience. It's always best to experience God's preventing power to keep us from sin rather than his intervening power to cleanse us from sin. That cleansing will purify our hearts but will not nullify the consequences of our actions.

In Israel's case, "the LORD turned from his fierce anger" (7:26). Many churches need to experience a turnaround. I wonder how many of those turnarounds might begin if leaders took the actions that would cause God to turn from his anger.

EXPERIENCING RESTORATION

Once the people of Israel completed the steps that removed deception—consecration, presentation, confession, and devotion—God restored them. The record of this restoration is found in Joshua 8.

Encouragement. Restoration began with a rekindling of courage: "Do not be afraid; do not be discouraged" (8:1). This same call was given to Joshua as he began his leadership role (1:9) and would be repeated later in the face of other leadership challenges (10:25). God knows that if leaders remain discouraged, their failures will be final.

Discouragement usually affects us in areas where we've once been defeated. Since Israel had been defeated by Ai, the thought of attacking them again was discouraging. So, God diverted their attention from that defeat to an earlier victory: "You shall do to Ai and its king as you did to Jericho and its king" (8:2). God noted a distinction between Ai and Jericho. Since Jericho was the first city conquered, the plunder was considered firstfruits and was to be completely devoted to God. Now that they had fulfilled that commitment by exposing Achan's sin and devoting the stolen articles, the plunder of Ai would be theirs to keep.

By God's grace, Israel's previous defeat became a platform for victory (8:2–7). They attacked the city again, this time planning to draw the men of Ai into an ambush. The plan worked, as the shameful retreat which was the evidence of their earlier loss (7:5) became a strategy for luring the army of Ai away from the protection of the city (8:6). When weaknesses are turned into strengths, it is evidence that God is at work.

Realignment. God's restoration of Israel resulted in a complete realignment of their faith. One evidence of that is the realignment of God's commands and Joshua's orders (8:8). God gave the mandate, and Joshua translated it into specific action. Deception leads us to question God's faithfulness; restoration brings renewed faith in the Lord's commands and an eagerness to obey.

Also, following Israel's defeat of Ai, Joshua led the people in worship (8:30–35). A service of worship can be the capstone for a restoration process. Joshua built an altar to make offerings and had the law of Moses copied onto stones. He positioned the people around the ark and had every word of the law of Moses read to them, including the promise of blessings for obedience and curses for disobedience. While we no longer build altars or carve stones, we can testify to our renewed relationship with God by offering our worship to him and by learning from his Word.

DECEPTION FROM THE OUTSIDE:
LACK OF DISCERNMENT

There is a second origin of deception. In the case of Achan, it came from inside the camp and began with the disobedience of God's people. It was self-deception, deception from within. Deception can also come from without. Joshua 9 tells the story of Israel's deception by the Gibeonites, a Canaanite people who tricked Israel into making a treaty with them. This episode did not begin with disobedience but resulted in it. The two situations may be contrasted this way:

DECEPTION FROM THE INSIDE ACHAN: JOSHUA 7	DECEPTION FROM THE OUTSIDE THE GIBEONITES: JOSHUA 9
Disobedience and Deception (7:1)	Deception (9:1–13)
Defeat and Destruction (7:2–5)	Disobedience (9:14–15)
Distance from God (7:6–12)	Disunity (9:16–21)

No matter what the source, deception debilitates God's people and inhibits their forward progress. Joshua's failure to respond prayerfully and carefully to the Gibeonites' offer resulted in deception rather than discernment.

For spiritual leaders, deception is a constant threat. Our ultimate enemy, Satan, is a deceiver by nature. His first interaction with the human race was an attempt to deceive Eve. His last interaction with the human race will be an attempt to deceive the nations (Rev. 20:7–8). So, we must constantly be on guard against not only self-deception, but also the deceptions of Satan.

To do that, we need discernment. We may gain that by understanding how the Gibeonites fooled Joshua and the leaders of Israel. Their failure to discern the truth provides a chilling lesson for us.

THE CORRUPTION OF DISCERNMENT

Discerning leaders are not deceived. Therefore, the first step in the deception of a leader is the corruption of his or her discernment. This insidious process has resulted in disobedience by more Christian leaders than we would care to remember. Here's how that process progressed with the leaders of Israel.

There Was an Emphasis on Appearance. The Gibeonites prepared an elaborate ruse by loading their donkeys with worn-out sacks and wineskins, wearing worn and patched clothing and sandals, and bringing a food supply of dry and moldy bread. That made it appear that they had come from a great distance, well beyond the boundary that God had established as the forbidden zone for peace treaties (9:3–6).

False appearance is the essence of deception. Satan masquerades as an angel of light, a wolf in sheep's clothing. Leaders must look beneath the surface. While we must not succumb to cynicism, neither can we be naïve. We must recognize there are two sides to every story and seek out both sides. Discernment means doing some digging.

They Were Easily Dissuaded from Their Initial Concerns. To their credit, the leaders of Israel were suspicious of the story they were told (9:7–8). Leaders often have a certain intuition about communication that doesn't quite ring true. They need to listen to that intuition. This would have been a great place for Israel's leaders to take a time-out and prayerfully process those concerns. That would have moved their suspicions from the level of personal intuition to spiritual discernment.

Business writer Jim Collins discovered that the ability to practice disciplined thought is a trait of great companies. He describes this as the "discipline to confront the brutal facts of reality, while retaining the resolute faith that you can and will create a path to greatness."[1] Faith does not ignore concerns. Rather, it fully investigates concerns without losing its focus on God.

This ability to confront reality is also a characteristic of good relationships among leaders. Greg Hawkins, executive pastor of Willow Creek Community Church in Illinois, has a productive relationship with senior pastor Bill Hybels. Hawkins says, "I can always count on Bill to say the tough things, to address the tough issues. I never have to wonder about what he is thinking. If he has something to say to me, he says it."[2]

It would be speculation to say that some of the leaders of Israel had stronger suspicions than others, but that is often the case when an organization faces the need for discernment. Those with the strongest suspicions must calmly and convincingly express them to the group. Those who don't share those suspicions need to listen carefully and openly to the concerns of others. Fully processing concerns is a mark of strength in a leadership team.

They Were Flattered by the Offer They Received. When the Israelite leaders asked questions of the Gibeonites, they answered evasively at first, saying only, "We are your servants." Since their ancestors had suffered as slaves in Egypt for so many years, the idea of having servants must have been flattering to the Israelites. That flattery opened the door to further deception (9:8–9, 11).

Pride is the enemy of discernment and the ally of deception. Flattery inflates the ego. The flatterer's compliments make him appear to be gracious, and it's difficult to ask tough questions of an apparently benevolent person. Joshua would have been wise to recognize that this offer had nothing to do with God's promise of land. The Israelites were never promised that they would have servants from faraway countries. Flattery may lead us to seek perks that God never included in his covenant with us.

A flattering offer should raise a red flag. It should motivate us to look carefully at the intentions of the person making the offer and the obligations we might incur on accepting it.

They Were Misled by the Spiritualization of the Situation. The Gibeonites furthered their deception by spiritualizing the situation (9:9–10). They indicated that their long journey had been motivated by "the fame of the LORD your God" (9:9). Then they recounted the past victories God had provided for Israel against the Egyptians and the Amorites. Deception is often wrapped in a most spiritual sounding package.

Spiritualizing is the effort to bolster a weak argument with religious language. It's baptizing a selfish desire with the words, "God told me." It's saying, "God's not present in our worship services like he used to be," when the real issue is the personal preference of music style. It's purporting that the church has "lost its sense of warmth and fellowship," when the problem is really a loss of personal attention. Deceivers often use spiritualization to mask self-interest.

They Were Misled by Their Senses. Deception is most powerful when it involves all the senses. The Israelites began to be deceived by what they heard (9:8–11). The deception was reinforced by what they saw (9:12–13). It even included their sense of taste (9:14). When physical senses become a substitute for spiritual senses, deception is certain.

Discernment is based on spiritual senses. The Bible repeatedly calls us to have spiritual eyes that see and ears that hear. The mark of a spiritually mature leader is the ability to grasp truths which can be discerned only spiritually. That requires the mind of Christ (1 Cor. 2:14–16).

They Failed to Pray Before Making a Significant Decision. The Israelite leaders "did not inquire of the LORD" (9:14) about the Gibeonites' treaty offer. Presumption replaced prayer (9:14–15). If Joshua had sought God in prayer, he might have been warned of the deception. If Joshua had led the other leaders in prayer, they, too, would have sensed that something was amiss.

Israel's disobedience deepened as they entered a treaty of peace with the Gibeonites and ratified it with an oath. Human alliance replaced dependence upon God. God had repeatedly warned his people against forming alliances with neighboring nations. He alone would deliver Israel. Sometimes making peace leads to a compromise that is nothing more than disobedience.

They Rushed Their Decision. Three days later, the Israelites received word that the Gibeonites were not distant travelers but nearby neighbors (9:16). What if Joshua had simply allowed a little time to pass before acting? A delay of just three days would have brought the truth to light.

Sometimes delaying a decision for even a short time makes all the difference. One of the reasons God sometimes moves slowly is to allow time for his people to discern what is really happening. Moving quickly increases the possibility of deception. There are rare occasions when quick action is warranted. More often, quick action is a substitute for careful preparation.

THE CONSEQUENCES OF DECEPTION

The Israelites eventually discovered that they had been deceived, but the consequences of their hasty action were already set. Deception from without is often uncovered very easily. The damage, however, may not always be undone. Here's the aftermath of Israel's failure to discern.

Their Disobedience Brought Disunity. Making peace with the Gibeonites (9:15) brought dissension among the Israelites (9:18). The whole assembly grumbled upon hearing that their leaders had struck an improper alliance (9:15–21). When leaders compromise by placating one faction inappropriately, they generally lose the support of faithful people.

Many churches have been divided by leaders who cater to various groups, trying to maintain peace and unity. Rather than leading with prayerful conviction, they become increasingly frenzied in their effort to meet competing demands.

Their Promises, Though Based on Deception, Had to Be Kept. Because the Israelites had ratified their treaty with an oath to God, they had to honor it, even though it was made under false pretenses (9:19–27). The leaders of Israel rightly insisted that they must live by their word. In fact, later in Israel's history, the failure to keep this promise resulted in a famine (2 Sam. 21:1, 4, 6). In this case, a deal was a deal.

Part of what makes deception so painful is that its consequences remain long after the lesson has been learned. If not careful, a leader who discovers that he or she has been deceived may resort to a victim mentality. I know some leaders who seem to focus only on what others have done to harm them, even in small ways. Generally, they ignore the role that they played in creating the situation, insisting that it's all the other person's fault. A victim mentality leads to bitterness and paralyzes us in the past. A vision mentality, one focused on what we can learn and change, propels us into a brighter future.

Churches as well as individuals can develop a victim mentality. I know of a church that has been hurt by the deceptive actions of a previous pastor. That pastor was wrong and has gone through a process of restoration. Yet the church continues to replay the pain of the past rather than learn what it can from that difficult experience and move on. The present pastor finds it impossible to communicate a vision for the future to this church that sees itself as a victim of the past.

Whatever destruction has been wrought in our lives by deception—either deception by self or deception by others—we must ask God to bring the necessary healing, learn the important lessons, and then allow the vision of a glorious future to emerge.

14

MAINTAINING MOMENTUM

Joshua 13:1—21:42

Momentum Builder	Momentum Buster
Momentum Builder	**Momentum Buster**
Momentum is developed by refusing to allow your skills to confine God's mission.	Momentum is drained by failing to manage personal limitations.

I was emotionally drained. We had just buried my friend, my hero, my mentor—my father. Sixty years of age seemed far too young for him to die. His death left me feeling empty, and the vacuum was expanded by my disappointment that God had not healed him. It required my total energy to fulfill the most basic responsibilities to my family and ministry.

Dad's death occurred at a time when our congregation was poised to take a huge step of faith. After years of cramming worshipers into an inadequately sized multipurpose building four or five times each weekend, we were set to build our new Celebration Center. The financial commitment

> "Trust is the lubrication that makes it possible for organizations to work."
>
> —WARREN BENNIS

was daunting, and a strong leader was needed to give the people both reassurance and confidence.

> "You then, my son, be strong in the grace that is in Christ Jesus. And the things you have heard me say in the presence of many witnesses entrust to reliable men who will also be qualified to teach others."
>
> —2 TIMOTHY 2:1-2

My grief and responsibilities as a leader collided at this pivotal point in my ministry. Would I take time out for personal recovery and perhaps miss a window of opportunity for construction of the Celebration Center? Or would I push ahead at who knew what risk to my spiritual and emotional health? Or was there a third possibility? Was it possible that these two realities were being used by God to create another option that was not yet apparent?

There are pivotal points in every leader's life. If successfully navigated, they result in personal growth and ministry expansion. But if the leader gets stuck at one of these hurdles, it places an artificial boundary on both his personal development and ministry.

JOSHUA'S TURNING POINT

The middle chapters of the book of Joshua seem at first to contain merely a routine record of the conquest of certain areas within the Promised Land and a listing of the inheritance for each tribe of Israel. But buried among these lists of places and names are the pivotal points in Joshua's life. None is more important than the one found in Joshua 13:1: "When Joshua was old and well advanced in years, the LORD said to him, 'You are very old, and there are still very large areas of land to be taken over.'"

Two realities collided in Joshua's life: his personal limitations and the scope of the remaining mission. The Lord pointed out to him the pivotal point that would redefine his ministry and shape the remainder of his life.

THE REALITY OF PERSONAL LIMITATIONS

The first reality was Joshua's personal limitations: "You are very old" (13:1). Estimates place his age at this point at ninety to one hundred years. Joshua's limitation was physical—age was catching up with him. With the advance of years come certain limitations. Several years ago, Jim Buick, then CEO of Zondervan Corporation, spoke to a leadership luncheon at our church. He had announced his retirement from Zondervan, which came in the midst of a reorganization that he had engineered. In the question and answer time following his presentation, he was asked what was next for him. He commented that he would be more of a mentor than a leader in the next season of his life because "generals don't go to war in the twilight of their lives." Jim was acknowledging the limits of age yet remaining engaged in a ministry fitting for his life stage.

Everyone faces personal limitations; age is only one of them. One of the most perplexing for me is a limited energy level. While I have bursts of energy for starting new endeavors, my overall battery is lower than that of most leaders with similar responsibilities. Many times I've asked God to raise my energy level, to help me get by on less than the eight hours of sleep I seem to require each night. He has left that limit in place.

The apostle Paul had a personal limitation, which he called a thorn in the flesh (2 Cor. 12:7–10). While we don't know the exact nature of this limitation, we do know that Paul asked that it be removed three times. The thorn remained, but his anxiety about it was replaced by confidence in God's grace to endure. Paul came to believe that this weakness would allow God's strength to develop in his life. The personal limitation would be used for God's glory.

Leaders encounter many personal limitations:

- Age
- Physical diseases or disability
- Diminishing mental capacities
- Special needs of family members
- Lack of resources, money, or energy
- Limited spiritual gifts or leadership skills

In some cases, the effect of a personal limitation can be minimized or mitigated but only rarely eliminated. I can raise my energy level by eating right and sleeping well. I can manage it by pacing myself and setting clear priorities. Even so, I can only progress so far before I reach biological boundaries.

An unhealthy response to the reality of personal limitations is denial. Denial creates a blind spot, causing the leader to conclude that everything is fine. Those that follow that leader usually know better, and the leader's denial erodes his or her credibility. Denial only deepens the impact of the limitation because a limitation must be acknowledged in order to be managed.

THE REALITY OF THE UNFULFILLED MISSION

The second reality Joshua had to face was the scope of the mission yet to be fulfilled: "There are still very large areas of land to be taken over" (13:1). In the verses that follow, God specified the regions that remained unconquered and the enemies who dwelled in them (13:2–5). The list must have left an aging Joshua feeling overwhelmed.

An unhealthy response to the reality of a vast remaining mission is to downsize the mission to fit within the leader's limited reach. Many churches are not growing while multitudes of people in the community around them are heading toward an eternity without Christ. The reason is not lack of facilities, money, or volunteers—though these may be the stated reasons. The real reason is that the leaders have put a lid on the mission so that they won't have to face their personal limitations. The God-sized vision entrusted to them is reduced to fit comfortably within their man-sized limitations.

Those two realities beg this question of Joshua and leaders today: What will you do about the vast remaining mission in light of your increasing personal limitations?

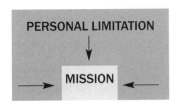

Most leaders face this dilemma more than once. As I look back over my life, I can identify at least a few such turning points. During these times of transition, God moves slowly to help the leader understand the reality of the situation and respond in a way that results in personal growth and ministry expansion.

Notice that God did not limit the mission to conform to Joshua's personal limitations. Instead, God reaffirmed his commitment to give Israel the whole Promised Land: "I myself will drive them out before the Israelites" (13:6). Then he asked Joshua to change his approach to leadership: "Be sure to allocate this land to Israel for an inheritance, as I have instructed you" (13:6).

Joshua could have reached this pivotal point and concluded that it was time for him to retire. It would have been easy to see his encroaching age as the end of his leadership. Or perhaps Joshua considered changing roles, finding it a challenge more in keeping with the abilities of an older man.

That's a choice made by many leaders who feel personal limitations placing a lid on their leadership ability. My first reaction when feeling my limits is to wonder whether it's time for me to move. At times, it is appropriate to change one's role or to fulfill the same role in a smaller setting. But often, God is not calling a limited leader to a new role but to a new responsibility within the current role. He's calling the leader not to go but to grow.

Joshua rightly saw this pivotal moment as a call to a new way of leading. Perhaps what God called Joshua to do is exactly what he wants most leaders to do at the pivotal points in their ministries: define, delegate, and develop. A leader defines the contribution he or she must make, delegates the achievement of the mission to other leaders, and then develops them to successfully fulfill their roles.

DEFINING YOUR ROLE

Every day, I pause for a moment during my quiet time with God to lay my calling before him. As I mentioned earlier, I ask him for three things related to my calling: clarity, intensity, and tenacity. That first request, for greater clarity, acknowledges my tendency to allow my sense of calling to get fuzzy. An ill-focused calling leads to diffusion of energy and loss of impact.

Most of us who serve as spiritual leaders find ourselves in an odd situation. We have been taught how to minister to others but not how to build our ministries. We can counsel other people but can't clarify our unique contribution. We can deliver a message to others but falter in giving direction to ourselves. This is a common situation and one we can manage with prayer and planning.

If we don't seek God for the design of our ministries, we will duplicate someone else's. This rarely works because God has given each of us different passions, gifts, and personalities. We try to be someone we are not. Like David who realized that King Saul's armor was ill-fitting and inappropriate for his mission to slay Goliath (1 Sam. 17:38–40), we, too, must understand ourselves and the ways God has gifted us to lead.

Here are some questions that have led to the clarification of my calling.

MINISTER VERSUS EQUIPPER

Am I a minister or an equipper? A minister is primarily a doer of ministry, someone who uses personal gifts to touch the lives of others. Ministers act directly—they preach sermons, give counsel, teach classes, make calls, and delight in being on the front lines with people. They relate readily to Paul's charge to Timothy: "Preach the Word; be prepared in season and out of season; correct, rebuke, and encourage—with great patience and careful instruction. . . . keep your head in all situations, endure hardship, do the work of an evangelist, discharge all the duties of your ministry" (2 Tim. 4:2, 5).

An equipper, on the other hand, is primarily a developer of other people and their gifts. Equippers minister indirectly—they prepare others to serve on the front lines of ministry. While they engage in some preaching or teaching, their first love is to develop others who have gifts in teaching, exhortation, and prophecy. Rather than making many calls themselves, they raise up a team of caregivers. Equippers often quote

Ephesians 4:11–12: "It was he who gave some to be apostles, some to be prophets, some to be evangelists, and some to be pastors and teachers, to prepare God's people for works of service, so that the body of Christ may be built up."

Is one right and the other wrong? One biblical and the other not? No. We each must understand who we are and then find a ministry setting that's conducive to living out that calling. Both ministers and equippers are used by God to build healthy churches. It is tragic that ministers sometimes disparage equippers—they label them as CEOs, saying that they are simply running a business. It's equally damaging when equippers take a condescending attitude toward ministers. That attitude is prevalent in the current ministry culture, where pastors who are doers at heart have felt marginalized and pressured to adopt the rancher approach to ministry.

Ministering and equipping are not exclusive of one another. Every equipper should continue some involvement in direct ministry. Every minister should equip others to do some of the work of the ministry. Each pastor needs to assess his or her passions, gifts, and temperament to determine which approach primarily characterizes his or her ministry.

As a rule of thumb, ministers are most effective in churches under three hundred people, where most of their schedule is filled with preaching, counseling, and calling. They tend to struggle when the congregation grows to the point that they can't keep up with the demands. Equippers tend to be more effective in larger churches, where parishioners more readily recognize that it is impossible for them to do most of the ministry and expect that it will be done through others. Equippers tend to struggle in settings where the majority of their ministry calls for one-to-one pastoral skills.

Someone who serves well as a minister may face the pivotal question: As I produce fruit in ministry and gain greater responsibility, will I move to a setting that allows me to continue serving as a minister, or will I become an equipper? Ministers who effectively preach God's Word and reach out to people through counseling, calling, and evangelizing will likely see growth in their churches. They may be called to a church when it averages one hundred in attendance, and their faithful ministry may build it to three hundred people. At that point, an equipper may be needed in order to produce continued growth. The pastor's dilemma: Should I become that equipper or should I go to another church of one hundred people and build it up?

When identifying your primary approach to ministry, be sure you don't have preconceived ideas about these roles. I attend a small group with a pastor I greatly admire. He has faithfully led a congregation for many years, leading it from a dysfunctional church on the brink of closure to a healthy congregation poised to break the two hundred attendees barrier. He is highly relational and loves investing time in people. Somehow, he was given the impression that in order to lead the church beyond two hundred, he would have to suppress his desire to relate to people and become primarily an administrator. In reality, he may simply need to focus his relational bent more intentionally on developing lay ministers who can then meet the needs of others. That would create a relational ripple that moved from him to other leaders to the congregation as a whole.

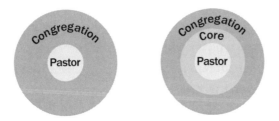

The next step for this pastor was not to become something he wasn't but to refine his greatest strength to accomplish a wider goal.

DOING VERSUS DELEGATING

What are the essential responsibilities I must fulfill and may not delegate to others? There are two steps to answering this question: One is to examine each responsibility to determine whether it should be done in the first place. As Peter Drucker says, "Nothing is less productive than to make more efficient what should not be done at all."[1] So, in order to answer this question, we must assess the present-day validity of our activities. It may be that a "not to do" list is more important than a "to do" list.

The second step in answering this question is to determine whether I am the one who should do the thing that should be done. Could others do it? Should others do it? When Kentwood Community Church was formed, there were many things that needed to be done, and I was the one who needed to do them. As the church increased the quality and quantity of its ministries, I did fewer things. Eventually, the board and I identified only three things as essential to my ministry—worship leadership, vision casting, and leadership development.

This question moves us from the assumption that everything is ministry to the discernment of the essential things in ministry. List the activities that currently fill your calendar. Identify the items that are essential and must be done. Identify which of these essentials you must not delegate and must do yourself.

ACCEPTING VERSUS DECLINING

What must I say no to? We may be able to accomplish anything we truly want in life, but we cannot accomplish everything. Successful leaders have learned to say no to opportunities that do not contribute to the mission to which God has called them.

The apostle Paul regularly left churches that loved him and would have welcomed his leadership for years to come. On at least one occasion, the church felt pain at his parting: "They all wept as they embraced him and kissed him. What grieved them most was his statement that they would never see his face again" (Acts 20:37–38).

Why would Paul say no to the opportunity to remain in leadership at a church that loved him and where there was so much yet to be done? His calling lay elsewhere. Romans 15:20 reveals Paul's mission: "It has always been my ambition to preach the gospel where Christ was not known, so that I would not be building on someone else's foundation." Paul was always moving on to the next city where a church planting project was needed.

Wayne Otto planted a church in Greenville, Michigan, and led it to become a thriving congregation that has greatly influenced that community. Under Wayne's leadership, the congregation grew to several hundred people, and there was tremendous potential for future growth. Yet he felt called to leave and start all over again in the nearby community of Ionia. The church in Ionia was no sooner launched when Wayne began dreaming of the next place where God would lead him. Do the churches in Greenville and Ionia have many good years ahead of them? Certainly. But by leaving, Wayne was saying no to something good in order to honor the calling God had placed upon his life.

When the choice is between good and bad, little discernment is required. When choosing between better and best, we must pray "to discern what is best" (Phil. 1:10). Saying no clarifies a vision more than saying yes. When you put your yeses and nos together, your sense of calling will be crystal clear.

List the opportunities that are currently before you. Rank them with one being best, two second best, and so on.

TRACKING GOD'S LEADING

Do I keep track of the occasions when God's Spirit has prompted me? I make entries into my journal on a daily basis. I record what I sense are God's promptings for my personal life, relationships, and pastoral leadership. The simple act of writing them down solidifies some of God's messages to me. Reading them later usually reveals themes that bring longer-term definition to my roles as a follower of Christ, husband, father, friend, and pastor.

"It's been estimated that 97 percent of business people do not set goals. Of this group, entrepreneurs are above average—more than 80 percent spend no time each day setting goals or planning, 15 percent spend up to [twelve] minutes, and only 5 percent spend at least [fifteen] minutes a day planning for themselves."[2] That means that while they work long and hard, their efforts are often unfocused and unproductive. What a loss!

But there is a greater loss which has eternal consequences. It's the failure of spiritual leaders to take time each day to ask God what he wants to say and do through them. What would the percentages be? Could it be said that 80 percent of Christian leaders spend no time each day praying for and mapping the leading of God's Spirit? This failure, repeated day after day, causes leaders to drift from God's design. It also confirms the reality so clearly communicated by Jesus: "If a man remains in me and I in him, he will bear much fruit; apart from me you can do nothing" (John 15:5).

I challenge you to lay your calendar before God each day. In a spirit of submission, pray through each appointment and activity. Seek his will for the blank spaces in that day's schedule, and fill them with prayer-prompted priorities.

DELEGATING RESPONSIBILITY

Delegation is a critical skill for any leader who wants to minimize the effects of a personal limitation and continue to pursue the mission. Having defined the personal contribution God calls us to make, we must delegate what remains to others. When Joshua divided the remaining territory among the tribes, he essentially delegated to other leaders the responsibility for conquering that land. Up to that point, there had been a centralized offensive with Joshua as its leader. Now, the battle would move forward under decentralized leadership.

Joshua moved from being a doer to a delegator. That may be a transition we are called to make as well. The more we become involved in equipping (versus ministering as defined earlier), the more indispensable is the art of delegation.

Why is delegation so difficult? The reason is partly practical. It often seems easier to do something myself than to teach another person to do it. But the reason goes deeper—delegation involves trust. Am I willing to trust others with not only the responsibility, but also the authority to carry out critical dimensions of the mission?

The development of trust requires a mutual contribution. The one who receives responsibility must be trustworthy. Faithfully discharging smaller responsibilities will lead to being entrusted with more

(Luke 16:10). The one who delegates authority must be trusting. And trust always involves risk, so the delegator must be willing to take a reasonable risk in order to provide an opportunity for someone else to succeed. As the one given responsibility achieves the desired result, a new level of trust is created, paving the way for even greater successes.

Three dimensions of delegation increase the likelihood of success.

DIMENSION ONE: DELEGATE RESULTS, NOT TASKS

God instructed Joshua to divide up the Promised Land among the tribes of Israel, giving the leaders of each tribe the responsibility to conquer that portion of property. Joshua did not prescribe how the tribes were to conquer their territory, only what territory to conquer.

If we delegate tasks, we simply tell people what to do. That keeps them dependent upon us. They go off to do their task, then return to us to report that the task is completed and receive another. If a problem arises, they return to us to solve it. While it may feed the ego to be the answer person, this is the least effective form of delegation.

On the other hand, if we delegate the results, we are specifying the goal to be accomplished, leaving it to the individual to determine how it should be done. As leaders, we provide a vision of what is to be accomplished. We also provide broad parameters of authority within which the mission must be fulfilled. Others then provide the strategies for accomplishing the vision within those broad-stroke boundaries. While some of their strategies may fail, this form of delegation empowers people to be successful independently. It develops them as leaders, not just doers.

When delegation does not produce the desired result, an initial response may be to fault the other person. We should resist that tendency and instead look at the content of our communication. If people don't understand what the desired results are and why they are important, they're likely to pursue different goals for different reasons. If we can't communicate the results we want, we will get the results we don't want.

DIMENSION TWO: CREATE SYSTEMS FOR SUCCESS

Every organization has systems that sustain its life and vitality. The church is called the body of Christ and is compared to a human body. A body has certain systems—such as circulatory, nervous, and reproductive—to sustain itself. In the same way, a local church must have certain systems to ensure good health.

The key to creating successful systems is to make them process dependent rather than people dependent. For instance, consider your system for assimilation, moving people being from first-time visitors to fully contributing members of your church. If your system depends on the heroic effort of a few uniquely gifted individuals, it will fall apart when those people are no longer involved. However, if your assimilation system has several clearly defined steps that involve a number of people at a level appropriate to their gifts, then assimilation will continue even after a change in leaders.

Kentwood Community Church had a person who was gifted in recruiting teams of people to serve in short-term mission endeavors. However, he did much of it personally and became the go-to person for any problem or question. The more successful he was in recruiting teams, the less effectively the system worked. It was person dependent. Once the steps of preparing for a mission trip were clearly identified and the desired results specified, many people could take a slice of the responsibility. The system became process dependent, which allowed for the delegation of responsibility to others.

DIMENSION THREE: DELEGATE AS MUCH AS POSSIBLE

When Joshua finished delegating, all the territory had been assigned to others. He did not leave any territory for himself to conquer. He gave away all of the authority and responsibility along with the territory. Many leaders set out to delegate results but end up with a long list of personal responsibilities. A leader must let people be responsible for their successes and failures. When people come to you for a solution, don't provide the answer. Ask them to diagnose the situation and arrive at a solution. Equip them to solve their problems. Once you have delegated everything, you will be free to do what is most important for a leader to do—identify new opportunities for mission fulfillment.

Personal insecurity causes us to cling unnecessarily to the achievement of results that can be obtained by others. To give it all away makes us feel vulnerable and dispensable. Yet if we devote that newly freed time and energy to achieving the next thing God calls us to do, we make a greater contribution to the mission.

DEVELOPING RESOURCES

Leaders who have defined their unique contribution and delegated the authority and responsibility for results are free to spend their time and energy developing the resources that are needed to fulfill the mission. The greatest of those resources is people. Some of those people are already serving faithfully alongside you. They need your blessing. Others will emerge under your leadership. They need encouragement.

BLESS EXISTING LEADERS

When Joshua was a much younger man, he was one of twelve commissioned by Moses to scout the Promised Land (Num. 13–14). Of the twelve, he was one of only two who brought back a positive report. Who was the other? A man named Caleb. It was Caleb who silenced the grumbling after everyone was disheartened by the negative report from the other ten spies. It was Caleb who expressed certainty that the Israelites could indeed take possession of the Promised Land (Num. 13:31). Caleb and Joshua were partners in giving a faith-filled report of the possibilities that lay before Israel.

Now, Joshua was very old and had to adopt a new approach to conquering the remaining territory of Canaan. Who would step forward to inspire others and provide an example of leadership? His old partner, Caleb. Forty-five years had passed, but Caleb was as anxious as ever to join Joshua in the quest to conquer the land: "I am still as strong today as the day Moses sent me out; I'm just as vigorous to go out to battle now as I was then. Now give me this hill country that the LORD promised me that day. You yourself heard then that the Anakites were there and their cities were large and fortified, but, the LORD helping me, I will drive them out just as he said" (Josh. 14:11–12).

Caleb was willing to take God at his promise and drive out whoever stood in his way. What an inspiration to the leaders of other tribes and clans.

What was Joshua's response to Caleb's request? Joshua blessed Caleb and gave him his inheritance. Joshua rightly recognized the presence of a proven leader. Caleb needed no training, only the freedom to do what God had called him to do.

In our eagerness to identify emerging leaders, we must not neglect existing leaders who have been faithful in the past and may well be chomping at the bit for a new challenge. This does not mean that we burden already busy people with meaningless activities. It means that we offer them new areas of ministry or new levels of opportunity within their current place of service. Offering leaders a new challenge frees them to act upon God's promises in courageous ways.

BUILD UP EMERGING LEADERS

When he assigned the unconquered territories to the various tribes and clans, Joshua was empowering their leaders to step up to a new responsibility. In so doing, he took leaders who had been faithful in a lesser responsibility—leading a tribe or clan—and gave them the opportunity to be faithful in something greater—conquering territory for the tribe or clan.

The Bible is realistic in portraying the various levels of success achieved by these emerging leaders. The leaders of the tribe of "Judah could not dislodge the Jebusites" from Jerusalem (15:63). The leaders of the tribe of Ephraim were not able to eradicate the Canaanites from Gezer but settled for making them do forced labor (16:10). These partial victories remind us that equipping leaders for new levels of responsibility is not a no-risk proposition.

Leaders are learners, and learning involves faith. Exercising faith involves risk, and risk implies the possibility of failure. When emerging leaders feel threatened by the possibility of retribution for failure, they become timid. They live within the comfort of the proven possible. They find ways to avoid performing so that they will not fail. But if they do not fail, they cannot learn. Emerging leaders need encouragement to continue on the right paths and coaching to identify and avoid wrong paths.

Richard Zalack, who has studied the role of the coach extensively, has identified four steps in successful coaching:

1. Communicate the expected result to team members.
2. Show them the result by achieving it yourself.
3. Watch them attempt to achieve the result.
4. Praise their success or redirect them back through the process.

All successful coaches, no matter what their field, follow these four action steps.[3]

Personally, I have found the most difficult part of coaching to be asking questions rather than providing answers. Answering questions may produce a solution, but asking questions produces leaders who create solutions on their own. Being the answer man may be good for my ego, but it's lousy for equipping. When someone encounters a problem and comes to me for the answer, I'm learning to ask questions rather than dispense advice. What are the options? What would be the results, intended or otherwise, from pursuing each option? Which option do you think is best? What could you do to make it better? Guiding leaders through the process of making decisions themselves is the best, long-term strategy for leadership development.

Sometimes emerging leaders want greater reward without accepting greater responsibility. Joshua encountered that attitude in the leaders of the people of Joseph (17:14–18). They rightly acknowledged that God had blessed them and made them numerous. They requested more territory based on this blessing. Joshua did assign additional territory to them, but it was occupied by the Canaanites, whom the Israelites found intimidating. When assigning the additional territory, Joshua reaffirmed that the Israelites were numerous. The blessing they had cited as a reason for seeking greater reward was the same blessing Joshua cited in challenging them to conquer more territory: "You are numerous and very powerful. . . . though they are strong, you can drive them out" (17:17–18). He wanted them to use their strengths to accomplish something, to further God's mission rather than demand an entitlement.

In both blessing existing leaders and empowering emerging leaders, the character of the subordinate leader is critically important. It's amazing how many spiritual leaders neglect the character issue when enamored with a young leader's experience or skills. It is far easier to teach skill to a person of character than it is to change the character of someone who is highly skilled: character first, commitment second, and competence third.

REACHING BEYOND THE LIMIT

In spite of Joshua's personal limitation, the vast remaining mission was accomplished:

> So the LORD gave Israel all the land he had sworn to give their forefathers, and they took possession of it and settled there. The LORD gave them rest on every side, just as he had sworn to their forefathers. Not one of their enemies withstood them; the LORD handed all their enemies over to them. Not one of all the LORD's good promises to the house of Israel failed; every one was fulfilled. (21:43–45)

Sometimes God moves slowly so that we will recognize our limitations and learn how to transcend them in order to fulfill our God-given mission.

15

THE CRUCIBLE OF CONFLICT

Joshua 21:43—22:34

Momentum Builder	**Momentum Buster**
Momentum is developed by faithfully engaging conflict.	Momentum is drained by failing to resolve conflict.

A board on which I served once dealt with a situation where a plateaued local church had called an energetic young pastor. The young man was initially greeted with enthusiasm, but before long, his changes found resistance among some long-term members. People chose sides and labels were applied. The situation escalated to the point where some members were perceived as winners and others as losers. In the end, the pastor remained as leader while many long-term members left the church. It could have easily ended the other way around. Sadly, ill-managed conflict resulted in division.

> "If passion drives you, let reason hold the reins."
> —BENJAMIN FRANKLIN

There are many surprises in the life of a spiritual leader. One of those surprises is how quickly a group of people can move from celebration to conflict. One day, they may communicate affirmation and the next day radiate suspicion. The distance between unity and disunity is incredibly short and all too easily, traveled.

> "Peacemakers who sow in peace raise a harvest of righteousness."
> —JAMES 3:18

Joshua saw that principle powerfully at work shortly after God declared the conquest of the Promised Land to be complete (Josh. 21:43–45). The conquest was made possible, in part, because the Reubenites, the Gadites, and the half tribe of Manasseh—who had been assigned territory on the east side of the Jordan—had fulfilled their promise to assist the other tribes in subduing the nations on the west side (22:1–9). Moses had assigned eastern territory to those two and a half tribes on the condition that they agree to do just that (Num. 32:16–33). Moses clearly communicated that condition to Joshua, Eleazar the priest, and the family heads of the Israelite tribes.

Now that the conquest was complete, Joshua publicly declared that the eastern tribes had fulfilled their commitment and sent them home with the plunder they had earned. They departed with the satisfaction of having kept their promise and the prosperity God bestowed upon their faithful labor. But by the time they reached the Jordan River, conflict erupted.

THE VALUE OF CONFLICT RESOLUTION

While most of us enjoy the celebrations of ministry, few of us enjoy the conflicts. Recognizing and resolving conflict is my Achilles' heel as a leader. Far too often, I've either created conflict or avoided it, leaving it unresolved. As I have learned more about conflict resolution and become better skilled at handling it, there has been greater unity within our staff members, lay leaders, and congregation.

One of the reasons God sometimes moves slowly is to allow for conflict resolution. This resolution can take a good deal of time, but if conflict is left unresolved, it will consume even more time and energy later on. Resolving conflict is a matter of paying now or paying more later.

There are two extreme views of conflict. One is that all conflict is harmful, even sinful. By this reasoning, conflict is to be avoided at any cost. That thinking causes many people to live in denial, ignoring the reality of conflict. Rather than true peace, it results in a cease-fire or truce. Conflict becomes the elephant in the room—everyone knows it is there, but no one will acknowledge it. Left unaddressed, conflict can become chronic, even terminal, for a movement of God.

The other extreme view is that all conflict is helpful. It is to be expected and embraced as a godly means of building up the fellowship of God's people. Every confrontation is seen as an opportunity to deepen relationships and develop the ministry. This thinking may cause some people to escalate conflict, needlessly expending time and energy that would be better devoted to higher causes.

The biblical view of conflict lies somewhere between these two extremes. It is displayed in verses like Colossians 3:13: "Bear with each other and forgive whatever grievances you may have against one another. Forgive as the Lord forgave you." This verse calls for forbearance so that not every difference of opinion is viewed as a conflict. It also calls for forgiveness in cases where the conflict is serious.

Forbearance is an old word but a good one. It reminds us that every perceived slight or rash word should not become a source of conflict. If every minor offense were viewed as a threat to a relationship, any group of people would tire of one another. "Bear with one another" is a biblical expression roughly equivalent to the maxim, "Don't sweat the small stuff, and most of it is small stuff."

There are times when conflict can be avoided with integrity. A meeting may become emotionally charged or a person may be defensive in a conversation. If a time-out is taken and an opportunity for reflection given, those involved will likely adopt an attitude of forbearance and conclude that their initial reaction was not the best response. Forbearance tempers raw emotion with spiritual wisdom.

Forgiveness is needed when an offense has gone deeper. The expression "forgive and forget" does not serve us well. To simply forget about a conflict is an act of forbearance. What we cannot forget must be forgiven. There are insults that are too painful or damaging to be avoided with integrity. To do so would be to shut down a part of our soul, creating fertile soil for the root of bitterness to take hold. When deeply wounded, we must come to the point of offering forgiveness; we must forgive as Christ forgave us. Forgiveness does not always lead to reconciliation. To fully recover a relationship depends on mutual participation in the process of conflict resolution. One person can forgive; it takes two to be reconciled.

The conflict that erupted between the tribes of Israel could not be avoided with integrity (Josh. 22:10–34). Although it was based on a misperception, this conflict showed that the tribes of Israel cared deeply about their unity and did not want a geographical boundary—the Jordan River— to become a relational or spiritual barrier between them. Conflicts probably occur more frequently where people care more deeply. "Conflict occurs most often in congregations in which there is a deep commitment to the church. The more deeply ingrained the sense of ownership about what is happening, the more possible is conflict. Apathy is a sure guarantee of a conflict-free setting. Persons who do not care about their faith are unlikely to exhibit enough energy to act upon it. Corpses do not fight!"[1]

The successful resolution of Israel's conflict would produce greater unity. The conflict had the potential, if not resolved successfully, to escalate into civil war, perhaps weakening Israel to the point that it could not maintain occupation of the Promised Land.

SOURCES OF CONFLICT

Conflict can arise from many different sources. Just as a medical doctor must make a diagnosis before writing a prescription, so the source of a conflict must be diagnosed before a resolution can be determined.

A brief survey of conflicts described in the New Testament reveals at least four sources.

SOURCE ONE: PERSONAL ISSUES

Conflict may begin within an individual who then projects his or her internal conflict upon an external situation. James poses this question: "What causes fights and quarrels among you? Don't they come from your desires that battle within you? You want something but you don't get it. You kill and covet, but you cannot have what you want. You quarrel and fight" (James 4:1–2). Troubled people cause trouble. A troublemaker is the opposite of a peacemaker.

Sometimes, I allow internal turmoil to spill into the situation around me. When that happens, someone who loves me will usually pull me aside and ask what's really bothering me. Initially, I may be defensive, but loving persistence eventually leads me to admit that my feelings are completely unrelated to the conflict. But some people are chronically troubled. They may have unresolved bitterness, untreated mental illness, or perhaps have given Satan a foothold in their lives through continual anger. There is a long list of possible reasons. These high-maintenance people create conflict wherever they go. They, too, must be brought to understand that the source of conflict is within them.

Willingness to look within is a mark of humility and paves the road to freedom. If a troubled person is unable or unwilling to examine internal conflicts, we, as spiritual leaders, must minimize the impact they have on others and marginalize their influence on the group. A troubled person should not be placed in a leadership role.

SOURCE TWO: PRIORITY DIFFERENCES

Conflict can occur when people have different priorities. This is not an issue of sin or selfishness but a genuine difference of opinion about where resources should be invested. This was the situation in Acts 6:1–7. The church was growing rapidly and had outgrown the apostles' ability to meet the needs of all believers. As a result, certain widows were being neglected in the daily distribution of food. The apostles decided that their first priorities should be prayer and the ministry of the Word of God. Yet they affirmed the validity of supporting widows and proposed that seven men "full of the Spirit and wisdom" (Acts 6:3) be chosen to handle the responsibility to distribute food.

This proposal was well-received by the whole group. Seven men were chosen, which resulted in an increase in the number of leaders. It also permitted the unhindered spread of the gospel, which resulted in an increase in the number of disciples in Jerusalem. This conflict was resolved by finding a way for the right people to address the priorities that would sustain this fresh movement of God.

Most growing movements experience a clash of priorities because they have limited resources of time, money, and energy. This type of conflict is predictable and can be very productive by stimulating involvement in the mission by others. Leaders are wise to avoid seeing priority conflicts as issues of right and wrong or spiritualizing the conflict. They do well to see such disputes as questions of timing and resources, and seek answers that promote all of the God-honoring priorities.

SOURCE THREE: PERSPECTIVE VARIANCES

Different people can look at the same person or situation and arrive at completely different conclusions. Such was the case with Barnabas and Paul, who couldn't agree on whether Mark should accompany them on another missionary journey (Acts 15:36–41). Mark had previously deserted them, not following through on his assignment. Barnabas, always the encourager, wanted to give Mark a second chance. Paul, who could never understand anything less than full devotion, thought it unwise to trust Mark a second time. The disagreement between Barnabas and Paul became so sharp that they eventually decided to go their separate ways.

Happily, that resulted in two missionary journeys instead of one. Barnabas took Mark and sailed for Cyprus. Paul was joined by Silas and traveled through Syria and Cilicia strengthening the churches. While Paul and Barnabas did not share the same perspective, neither did they disparage one another. In fact, near the end of his life, Paul had seen such a change in Mark and had come to appreciate him so much that he asked for Mark to attend him during his final days (2 Tim. 4:11). Was Barnabas right and Paul wrong? That's not the issue, and it seldom is in resolving conflicts of perspective. Resolution depends on maintaining respect for those who hold a different view while continuing to work—perhaps separately—for the advance of the gospel. Sometimes it's best to agree to disagree, then shift attention from the dissension to the mission.

SOURCE FOUR: PRINCIPLE OFFENCES

Principle-centered conflicts can occur when one person has sinned against another. Jesus described the process for resolving these conflicts, instructing us to approach the offending party and point out the fault. If that person responds, the conflict is solved. If the person will not listen, however, we are to enlist the aid of another person or two and try again to resolve the situation. If the person still refuses to respond, then the matter is to be brought before the church for action (Matt. 18:15–17).

If someone comes to me to discuss a situation where another person has sinned against him, at the earliest possible moment in the conversation, I ask whether he has confronted that person already. If the answer is no, I make it clear that confronting that person personally is his next step. I then offer to pray for the situation, asking God to give a clear voice and a listening ear. If the situation is really based on a misunderstanding, I ask God to bring that to light so that both parties can see it. I also pray that the offending person will have a responsive heart and, if the situation calls for it, a repentant spirit. Only after the initial step of personal confrontation would a conflict resolution team become involved in seeking resolution.

Principle-centered conflict may involve a group of people as opposed to two individuals. When a principle is at stake, it must be publicly discussed and resolved. Such was the case in Acts 15 when the Jerusalem Council met to discuss the role of Jewish law in the lives of Christians. Some Jewish Christians argued that Gentile Christians should observe the law as a sign of their true acceptance of Christ—circumcision, as taught by Moses, was a requirement for salvation. Others, notably Paul, disagreed. They believed that, in Christ, we are free from the requirements of the law. Conflict arising from differing value systems is the deepest and most difficult kind. People will kill and be killed for principles they see as nonnegotiable.

At the Jerusalem Council, background information was openly presented. Then the apostles and elders met to consider the issue. Finally, Peter, who spoke with great authority to Jewish Christians, announced the council's decision—a compromise which allowed Gentiles to come freely to Christ but asked that they defer to Jewish sensibilities on certain matters. The council's open approach to resolving this dispute avoided discord while preserving the central value of Christianity— salvation through faith in Christ alone.

RESOLVING CONFLICT

The conflict that unfolded in Joshua 22 sprang from two sources: perspective and principle. It is not unusual to have two or more sources of conflict overlapping in one event.

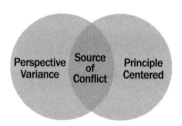

Conflict arose when the eastern tribes built an imposing altar near the Jordan River (Josh. 22:10). Ever since the encampment at Sinai, the Israelites had a centralized place of worship, the tabernacle. The construction of alternate places of worship was expressly forbidden by God. The western tribes viewed this act of devotion by their kinsmen as a violation of God's command. What was intended as a declaration of unity was misinterpreted as an act of rebellion.

The process by which this conflict was resolved yields helpful guidelines for resolving most conflicts that involve a group of people.

STEP ONE: SELECT A TEAM (JOSH. 22:13–14)

First, a representative group from the western tribes was selected to initiate communication with the eastern tribes. When a conflict involves a large group of people, it's usually best to refer it to an appropriate team of people. The role of that team must be carefully defined. Will it be to facilitate discussion only, to make a recommendation, or to decide on a resolution? In Israel's case, the team was commissioned to seek an interview and report back on the reason behind the eastern tribes' construction of the altar.

The team was led by a spiritual leader—Phinehas the son of Eleazar the priest. Its membership included ten chief men, one from each of the nine and a half western tribes, so it was a representative group. Representatives must represent the whole group not just their interest group. And they must be qualified to contribute to the process, not chosen merely to get a representative from each tribe.

Referring conflict to a team may prolong the process of resolution, but it may also diffuse the tension. When the western tribes heard about the altar, they mobilized for war against the eastern tribes. Their first impulse was to do battle. The time it took for the team to do its investigative work provided a cooling-off period when calmer minds could prevail. Using the team method can move a conflict from an emotionally charged setting to a more rational footing, which is especially helpful during the information gathering phase.

The best team members do not take conflict personally; they are not paralyzed by the thought of being personally disliked or having their ideas rejected. Peacemakers must be patient with a process that can be highly ambiguous and frustrating. They must also be neutral, entering the situation without a personal agenda, in order to have credibility with all sides involved.

STEP TWO: COMMUNICATE CONCERNS (JOSH. 22:15-18)

The team appointed by the western tribes entered an emotionally charged situation where they communicated their concern by asking questions. Those questions belied their assumptions, which was not an ideal tactic. Their questions began in an accusatory manner but ended by showing at least some willingness to listen:

- "How could you break faith with the God of Israel like this?" (22:16).
- "How could you turn away from the LORD and build yourselves an altar in rebellion against him now?" (22:16).
- "Was not the sin of Peor enough for us?" (22:17).
- "And are you now turning away from the LORD?" (22:18).

During this information gathering phase of their conflict resolution, the team attempted both to clarify their position and to understand the perspective of the eastern tribes. The first two questions clarified their position. The third question cited a historical precedent for their concern, referring to a time when some Israelites became involved in an inappropriate form of worship. The last question inquired into the motivation behind the eastern tribes' action.

Because the eastern and western tribes were on the brink of battle, the questioning phase was crucial for avoiding unhealthy fighting by either side. By asking questions, the western tribes initiated a healthy problem resolution strategy that would provide the freedom to arrive at a solution.

Healthy conflict resolution begins with communication. Each side must make a clear statement of the need or goal behind its concern. The more ways in which that communication is given, the more likely it is to be understood.

STEP THREE: CONCEPTUALIZE POSSIBLE OPTIONS (JOSH. 22:18-20)

The western group clearly communicated the fact that they saw the construction of this altar as a matter that would affect the entire nation of Israel (22:18). They cited the sin of Achan to illustrate the point

(22:20). They reminded their brethren of the fact that God looked upon them as one nation not as separate entities divided by a river. If judgment was to come, it would come upon all. By defining the danger as all-inclusive—it would affect the eastern and the western tribes—they avoided casting the debate in us-versus-them terms.

Then they offered a solution to the eastern group that demonstrated a willingness to sacrifice: "If the land you possess is defiled, come over to the LORD's land, where the LORD's tabernacle stands, and share the land with us" (22:19). Although the land west of the Jordan had been apportioned to the nine and a half tribes, they were more than willing to share it with the other two and a half tribes in order to prevent any inappropriate worship and the judgment it would surely bring. The western tribes probably felt that they were offering a superior property to the eastern tribes because God had clearly identified the Promised Land as west of the Jordan. Their offer reflected the gracious spirit that is necessary in diffusing any conflict.

Though they had been ready to make war, the western tribes' make-them-pay attitude gave way to a let-us-help spirit. The movement from an us-versus-them to a we're-in-this-together mentality always creates a climate conducive to conflict resolution.

STEP FOUR: LISTEN TO THE RESPONSE OF THOSE CONFRONTED (JOSH. 22:21–29)

After offering a solution, the western tribes allowed the others to respond. They began by reaffirming their commitment to the shared value system of the Israelite tribes. They did this in three ways. First, they acknowledged the rightful place of their mighty God and gave him praise. Next, they affirmed that God understood their true motivation for building the altar—it was not an act of rebellion or disobedience (22:22). Third, they agreed that if their motive had been a rebellious one, the western tribes would have been warranted to take action. This demonstrated their willingness to be accountable for their actions (22:23).

Having established that common ground, the eastern tribes provided the explanation for their action. First, their motive was to prevent future generations from viewing the Jordan River as a spiritual barrier (22:24–25). The altar was intended as a symbol of solidarity with the main body of Israelites. Second, the altar was not a place for making sacrifices but a reminder that the eastern tribes worshiped the same God and should always have access to the sacrificial altar located on the western side of the river (22:26–28). Third, the altar was intended to be a permanent reminder that there was only one acceptable place to make burnt offerings and that all the people of Israel should have access to it (22:29). All of these explanations support the statement by the eastern tribes that their true motive was to honor God.

From our vantage point, mistaken assumptions created this conflict. The western tribes assumed that the altar had been constructed for burnt offerings—it hadn't. The eastern tribes assumed that future generations of western Israelites would use the geographical boundary of the Jordan against them—there is no objective reason to believe they would have. If either side had communicated clearly before the altar was constructed, there would have been no conflict.

As they talked and listened to one another, both groups communicated in emotion and action. They went beyond simply reporting the facts—which is vitally important—to communicating their feelings. Both the content (what happened) and the context (how we feel about it) must be communicated if reconciliation is to take place.

STEP FIVE: DETERMINE IF THE RESPONSES ARE CREDIBLE (JOSH. 22:30–33)

Phinehas and the other leaders were pleased by what they heard (22:30). They recognized the hand of God in the conflict resolution process and were convinced that the conclusion honored him (22:31).

The western delegation then completed their assignment. Since they had been commissioned to communicate concerns and report back, they returned home to make their accounting. Upon hearing the report, the whole assembly was pleased and used the occasion to give glory to God (22:32–33).

STEP SIX: BRING CLOSURE (JOSH. 22:34)

The eastern tribes brought closure to this conflict through a symbolic act. They named the altar "A Witness Between Us that the Lord is God" (22:34). It was a long name, but it addressed all the concerns of both parties to the conflict. For the eastern tribes, it provided a reminder that all Israelites must have access to the altar of sacrifice in Canaan. For the western tribe, it affirmed that the altar was intended to be a symbol, not a place of worship. For all the tribes, it publicly declared that "the Lord is God," putting them on record against the pagan practice of worshiping many gods in many places.

We rarely terminate our conflicts today by erecting or naming altars. But there are other spiritually significant symbolic acts that can seal the resolution of a dispute. What if all sides observed Communion together? Or participated in a foot-washing service or time of prayer around the altar? Wouldn't it be refreshing if all parities made a common statement affirming their shared values and conclusions? In these or other symbolic ways, we add a vertical dimension to conflict resolution.

Celebrating the fact that the conflict is ended may also be helpful. That celebration might take the form of a shared meal, a praise service, or the offering of affirmation to those who took part in the resolution. Celebration serves not only as a source of encouragement for those involved, but also as a witness to others who may have observed the dispute.

These steps to conflict resolution work best when taken in order. It's tempting to jump ahead, discussing options before the concerns are clearly identified, or declaring closure before true resolution has been reached. Slow-motion times allow us to follow the process carefully, all the way to completion.

16

A LEADER'S LEGACY

Joshua 23-24

Momentum Builder	**Momentum Buster**
Momentum is developed by leading well until you leave well.	Momentum is drained by failing to plan for transition.

Imagine giving your farewell speech. Not just a farewell speech at the conclusion of your career, but a farewell speech that publicly concludes your life. The last two chapters of Joshua record such a speech. Joshua's words cause me to reflect on what my words will be when the time comes for my farewell.

Final words make a lasting impression. I heard of one church where the pastor used his final sermon to preach on the evils of playing cards. It might have been a hot-button issue for him, but that hardly ended his

> "Things which matter most must never be at the mercy of things which matter least."
>
> —JOHANN WOLFGANG VON GOETHE

ministry with a life-changing message. We don't want to waste final words by majoring on the minors.

> "Now there is in store for me a crown of righteousness, which the Lord, the righteous Judge, will award to me on that day— and not only to me, but also to all who have longed for his appearing."
>
> —2 TIMOTHY 4:8

Nor should we use final words to settle a score. Many embittered leaders have used their farewell speech as an occasion to blast their enemies, real or imagined. That venting may provide a momentary sense of victory, but it seldom benefits leaders or endears them to the audience. Farewell speeches are best used to lay a foundation for the future, not recount the frustrations of the past.

The Bible records several farewell speeches. Many passages in both the Old and New Testaments are given to such orations. The fact that they are recorded in Scripture indicates their importance. At the ripe old age of one hundred ten, Joshua delivered his final address to the leaders of Israel. The centerpiece of the speech is often quoted: "Choose for yourselves this day whom you will serve . . . But as for me and my household, we will serve the LORD" (Josh. 24:15). There's a lot to learn from the rest of the speech too.

The speech provides an outline that may help us do some advance work on our farewell presentations, even though they may not be delivered for years to come. Yet I know that if my farewell speech is a work in progress, I'll be more likely to focus attention on the legacy I want to leave. That future focus will help me make decisions about how I want to live today.

Maybe that's another reason God sometimes chooses to move slowly. Rarely do urgent items form the core of one's legacy. Only when we take time for reflection, seeking a release from daily routines, do the items of highest importance come into view.

THE DATE OF DELIVERY

Most of us do not know when we'll give our farewell speech. Maybe we'll never have the chance to deliver it. Perhaps someone will discover our rough drafts and refine them for those we love. For Joshua, the delivery date came at an enviable time, when his personal limitations had finally caught up with him and the final chapter of his mission had been written.

Joshua completed the task God had given to him. As the book of Joshua opens, Moses had recently died and God gave Joshua this commission: "Be strong and courageous, because you will lead these people to inherit the land I swore to their forefathers to give them" (1:6). When he gave his farewell speech, Joshua's task was completed: "A long time had passed and the LORD had given Israel rest from all their enemies around them" (23:1). There was still work to be done, but Joshua's part was over.

One of my favorite verses is: "I have brought you glory on earth by completing the work you gave me to do" (John 17:4). Jesus, too, had accomplished his God-given mission. True, he had gathered only a handful of immature disciples, while the entire world was yet to be reached, but Jesus had the satisfaction of knowing that his mission was accomplished. He would make the transition to a ministry of intercession for others, those who would take up the mission from that point forward.

I went to lunch recently with some other pastors. One of them spoke of his sincere struggle to discern whether his present ministry assignment had been completed and the time was right to say farewell. He was considering his season in life, the complexity of his church's ministry, and the opportunities and obstacles that lay just ahead. He commented on the many times of prayer he had spent in seeking the will of God. Just then, another in the group piped in about a nearby pastor who had resigned abruptly out of frustration with his congregation. He gave no advance notice to the board or the leaders in his denomination. He announced his resignation on a Sunday morning, and it was effective immediately. I found myself wanting to handle my farewell like the first pastor, not the second. A departure should be prompted by prayerful reflection, not overwhelming frustration.

Joshua arrived at this "mission accomplished" point just as his personal limitations asserted their grasp upon his life. He was "by then old and well advanced in years" (Josh. 23:1) and said so to his leadership team (23:2). Joshua's energy for leadership had been spent. He understood that his capacities were diminishing.

We probably all know leaders who've stayed too long. Some even feel entitled to years of mediocre ministry as a reward for earlier years of productivity. They coast along, reciting their accolades from years gone by. They remain in the position but no longer have passion or fulfill the function. The respect they earned in earlier years is forfeited by their lack of discernment about their diminished capacities.

Joshua's limitations were acknowledged, and his assignment was completed. It was the right time to say good-bye. Joshua was about to die, and every promise that God made to him on behalf of the people of Israel had been fulfilled.

FACETS OF THE FAREWELL

Joshua's good-bye is a classic. Any leader who wants to begin crafting a farewell address, a statement of the legacy he or she wishes to leave, would do well to use it as a model. Joshua's speech offers seven points that are important to include in any farewell. It prompts me to ask seven questions about the end of my ministry.

BLESSINGS

What will I count as blessings at the end of my career? Joshua recalled all the benefits the Israelites had received as a result of the Lord's faithfulness (23:3). By doing so, he pointed out what they themselves had witnessed and gave glory to God for these good things. Looking back with gratitude would enable Israel to look ahead in faith. Past blessings generate confidence in future endeavors.

At one conference, I had conversations with two lay leaders who had left churches in order to serve God in new places. In the first, the lay person spoke highly of those with whom he had served at his previous church. He detailed some of the accomplishments they had achieved together. I left the conversation admiring his positive view of the past and his passion for the future. The second conversation was tinged with bitterness. The lay leader's condescending attitude left me with the impression that he considered the previous church to be beneath him. I left that conversation grateful that he was not part of our church—I was sure that sooner or later we would fail to measure up to his expectations. When someone blesses his past, I admire him. When someone bashes his past, I find myself wanting to avoid serving with him.

I don't advocate viewing life through rose-colored glasses. Anyone involved in the hard work of spiritual leadership knows that there are downsides as well as upsides. In spite of that, intentionally counting one's blessings acknowledges God's greatness and affirms his people.

UNFINISHED WORK

Joshua's speech prompts a second question for the close of a ministry. What work is yet to be done? A common trait among leaders is that they are able to see what is yet to be done. The leadership gift includes the ability to recognize goals that are still to be reached and problems yet to be solved. That contributes to the loneliness of leadership; the leader sees what others don't. Joshua used part of his farewell address to remind the Israelites of the land yet to be taken and the enemies yet to be conquered. He also reminded them that God's power would drive these enemies out; God's promises would be fulfilled (23:4–5).

Retiring leaders offer a gift to their successors when they identify the challenges that remain. They demonstrate humility when they avoid giving the impression that everything worth doing has already been done. That gives emerging leaders the opportunity to make a contribution. The next generation can then do more than maintain the glory of the good old days. They can build on the foundation that has been laid.

When stepping out of leadership, it's important to consider both the blessings of the past and the challenges of the future. If a leader considers only the blessings, it's easy for complacency to take root. If a leader considers only the challenges, there is no celebration of past accomplishments and therefore no momentum generated for new ones.

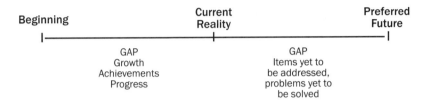

CHALLENGES

How will I challenge others to fully obey? Joshua discovered the personal benefits of fully obeying God. He was not a perfect leader, but he had been largely successful in responding to God's command: "Be strong and very courageous. Be careful to obey all the law my servant Moses gave you; do not turn from it to the right or to the left, that you may be successful wherever you go" (1:7). We hear the ring of that challenge in Joshua's final words to the people of Israel: "Be very strong; be very careful to obey all that is written in the Book of the Law of Moses, without turning aside to the right or to the left" (23:6).

Joshua was explicit about what disobedience (turning to the right or left) would look like for them. He named the sins to which they would be most susceptible. He warned against associating with the nations that remained in the Promised Land. He forbade the worshiping or serving of their gods, or even the mention of their names in making an oath. He banned alliances and intermarriage with other nations so that the Israelites would remain purely and fully dependent upon their God (23:7, 12).

Joshua made it clear that in order to obey, the Israelites must "hold fast to the LORD [their] God" (23:8).

RESOURCES

A fourth leadership question prompted by Joshua's farewell speech is this: What is the greatest resource for significant living? There are many resources that enrich the life of a leader. Educational opportunities can greatly enhance one's skills. Financial resources can provide experiences that refine or refresh. Good relationships are a resource that grants access to the wisdom and support of others. Acknowledging these resources not only increases our gratitude but also raises our awareness of how they might be managed effectively.

Joshua's farewell speech included a reminder of Israel's greatest resource—God, who fought for them (23:9–11). Because he was on their side, no one had been able to withstand them. A single Israelite had the ability to dispel a thousand of the enemy. We gain tremendous energy from joining God in something he has decided to do. No other resource can compare to his power.

In the Old Testament, the bestowal of God's power and presence was often called an anointing. It was the recognition that God had empowered a particular person for a particular task. That anointing could have been given for religious service, as in the case of a prophet or a priest. Or it might have been given for national service, as in the case of a king. When the favor of God rested upon a person, no human obstacle or liability could stand in the way.

Joshua experienced this anointing, and the leaders around him shared in it. This resource, Joshua advised, would continue to be available for as long as they loved the Lord their God (23:11). To love God completely is the fulfillment of the Great Commandment and the doorway to a life anointed by God.

PROMISES

Joshua's speech prompts me to ask a fifth question about the latter part of my leadership: What are the promises to be kept? Joshua reminded Israel's leaders of their covenant with God. Most covenants contained a historical prologue—a record of the events leading up to the making of the covenant. In his farewell speech, Joshua recounted the historical prologue to Israel's covenant with God (24:1–13). This brief history provided the context for God's present work. Hearing a bit of history reminds us that we only have one place in time; God's plan preceded us and will continue after us. Taking possession of the Promised Land fulfilled a covenant that God first made with Abraham and then with Moses. The people of Israel were reminded that it was their turn to live up to the promises of the ancient covenant, fully confident that God would always live up to his part of the bargain.

So Joshua called the people to make a decision: "Choose for yourselves this day whom you will serve" (24:15). It was necessary for each generation to affirm its commitment to abide by the covenant. Joshua reminded them that the choice was theirs. They could affirm their covenant with the Lord, serving him with all faithfulness. Or they could make a covenant with other gods, like those served by their ancestors or those worshiped by the inhabitants of Canaan.

Joshua indicated his choice in perhaps the most quoted verse in the book of Joshua: "But as for me and my household, we will serve the LORD" (24:15). Like any good leader, he invited the people to follow his example. The apostle Paul did much the same when he invited others to follow him as he followed Christ (see 1 Cor. 11:1). A leader incarnates full devotion to God.

The people respond to Joshua by affirming their desire to obey the Lord their God (Josh. 24:16–18). They recognized that it was God who delivered and protected them in the past. He had been their God and would continue to be.

Joshua's response to their affirmation is not what I would have expected. Rather than cheering them on, he flatly stated that they were unable to do what they said. Joshua predicted they would not keep their promises to God and there would be consequences for the inevitable break of their allegiance to him (24:19–20). That was hardly a motivational speech. Yet the people repeated their choice, agreeing to throw away their false gods and yield their hearts fully to the Lord. They witnessed their choice by erecting a stone monument (24:22–27). The goal was not outward conformity to the stipulations of the covenant; it was nothing less than the complete devotion of their hearts to God.

Why did Joshua focus the challenge of his farewell address on the people's covenant with God? Because the covenant was a vivid reminder that life is not, ultimately, about the relationship between people and their leader. It is about the relationship between people and their God. Good spiritual leaders faithfully shepherd their people and develop close bonds with them. Yet they constantly remind them that their primary allegiance is to God, not the leader. Leaders come and go. God is the same yesterday, today, and forever. Only he can give lasting significance to life.

LIFE SUMMARY

What statement will summarize my life and ministry? Once the people had confirmed their covenant choice (24:21–22), Joshua sent them away. Soon after that, he died. Scripture records this epitaph for Israel's great leader: servant of the Lord. Just as Moses before him had been called the Lord's servant, so Joshua received this honored description. Short but eternally significant, that may be the best memorial a spiritual leader could hope for.

My accountability partner has a custom license plate on his car. The message consists of the letters TKASG. Those letters represent his life's mission: to know and serve God. He is a devoted husband and father, a successful businessman, and one who consistently orders his life around eternal priorities. Yet he uses that simple phrase to maintain his focus on the real bottom line—knowing and serving God.

What statement will best describe your life and ministry? When I think about that question, I try to imagine the answer from God's perspective because it's his "well done, good and faithful servant" (Matt. 25:23) that I'm living for. Whatever statement you choose to live by, it should be a statement that captures both your character and calling.

For several years, I've used a self-assessment tool called a life arrow. This process, using the shaft of an arrow as a model, helps me to identify the people who have shaped me, the opportunities that have stretched me, the resources that have supported me, and the problems that have refined me. The tip of the arrow is a brief statement of what I hope these forces in my life will lead to. That summary statement helps me focus on the legacy I hope to leave rather than the obstacles encountered along the way.

SUCCESSOR

The last question for leaders prompted by Joshua's farewell speech is based on something he didn't say: Who are the leaders who will come next? If Moses passed the baton of leadership to Joshua, to whom did Joshua pass it? Did Joshua fail to make a transfer of power? Did he opt for leadership by committee ("the elders who outlived him" are referred to in Josh. 24:31)? Did Joshua think that having the land would be a substitute for having a leader?

There is no lasting success without successors. The passing of a long-term leader often results in a leadership vacuum. That can usually be avoided by careful succession planning. The first step in a succession plan may be to determine what form of leadership will be appropriate for the next stage in a movement of God. Perhaps Joshua sensed that decentralized leadership would be needed to settle the Promised Land. God often uses a dynamic person early in the development of an initiative, then uses a team of people to manage the results of that venture.

The second step in a succession plan is to define the process by which the new leader or leaders will be selected. I assisted our church board in developing a succession plan to be used for selecting the leader(s) who would come after me. Because I had served as senior pastor for nearly three decades, very few of our members had witnessed a succession in that role. By constitution, I did not select the leader who followed me. Yet I did want the process to be clearly understood so that definite steps could be taken at that critical juncture.

Parts of the plan were a bit unsettling to write. What would happen if I were to fail morally? What would happen if I didn't think it was time for me to leave but the congregation did? Thinking through various negative scenarios strengthened my resolve to ensure that they never come true. The plan specified what actions were to be taken, where the authority would rest, and who should be consulted in each case. The plan was reviewed on an annual basis by our board and was available to the congregation. Knowing that the possibility of succession had been considered and planned for provided a sense of assurance for our leaders.

It's my habit to follow a daily schedule for Bible reading so that I read the entire Bible in one year. Every time I read the books of Kings and Chronicles, I am disheartened to read of all the kings who started well but didn't finish well. One translation describes a few of them this way:

Uzziah. "So he became very famous, for the Lord helped him wonderfully until he was very powerful. But at that point he became proud—and corrupt" (2 Chron. 26:15–16 TLB).

Joash. "Joash tried hard to please the Lord all during the lifetime of Jehoida the priest. . . . But after his death the leaders of Judah came to King Joash and induced him to abandon the Temple of the God of their ancestors, and to worship shameful idols instead!" (2 Chron. 24:2, 17 TLB).

Jehoshaphat. "But at the close of his life, Jehoshaphat, king of Judah, went into partnership with Ahaziah, king of Israel, who was a very wicked man" (2 Chron. 20:35 TLB).

Reading about these men reminds me that spiritual leaders are never beyond temptation. I recall the wise words of one pastor I know whose son asked him to promise that he would never fall morally. The pastor responded, "Son, I can never guarantee that I will not fall. I can only assure you that I'll start every day on my knees, humbly asking God to give me the strength and grace I need to obey him in that day. I'll do that day after day until I draw my last breath." A daily affirmation of obedience leads to a lifetime of faithfulness.

I sometimes said to members of our staff, "Let's live our lives fully for the Lord. Someday we'll sit on a porch in our rocking chairs, sipping lemonade, and recall what a joy it has been to serve God our whole lives. We'll talk about the victories won and the lessons learned." There could be nothing simpler and sweeter.

I once attended a creative arts conference with nine of our staff, lay musicians, dancers, dramatists, and visual artists. I had the privilege of praying for them as the conference drew to a close. As the ten of us joined hands, I asked that God would protect us, that all of us would honor him all of our lives, and that someday, on some earthly or heavenly porch, we'd be able to share the joy of having served him until we went to be with him.

That's my prayer for you as well.

NOTES

CHAPTER 1

1. Carl F. George and Warren Bird, *How to Break Growth Barriers: Capturing Overlooked Opportunities for Church Growth* (Grand Rapids, Mich.: Baker Books, 1993).
2. Lyle E. Schaller, *Growing Plans* (Nashville: Abingdon Press, 1983).
3. Robert D. Dale, *To Dream Again* (Nashville: Broadman Press, 1981), 107.

CHAPTER 2

1. Price Pritchett, *Firing Up Commitment During Organizational Change: A Handbook for Managers* (Dallas: Pritchett Publishing, 1994), 5.
2. The mission statement and key result areas shared here are different from the mission and vision statements that currently guide our church. Our new mission and vision statements were the result of a strategic planning process we went through in 2000 and 2001, and are included in my book *Lead On: Why Churches Stall and How Leaders Get Them*

Going (Indianapolis, Ind.: Wesleyan Publishing House, 2003). Many of the core concepts expressed in the mission statement and key result areas here were carried forward into the new statements.

I'm convinced it's healthy for a church to annually review its mission and vision in order to make slight adaptions to it. I'm also convinced it's healthy for a church to consider a complete rewrite of its mission and vision every five to ten years. To make substantial changes too early or too often risks creating confusion. To never make substantial changes risks a lack of relevance to the world and a lack of ownership among those currently leading the church or ministry.

3. Warren G. Bennis and Burt Nanus, *Leaders: Strategies for Taking Charge* (New York: Harper & Row, 1985).

CHAPTER 3

1. Stephen R. Covey, *The 7 Habits of Highly Effective People* (New York: Simon & Schuster, 1989).
2. Ray and Anne Ortlund, *You Don't Have to Quit* (Nashville: Thomas Nelson, 1988).

CHAPTER 4

1. J. Robert Clinton, *The Making of a Leader: Recognizing the Lessons and Stages of Leadership Development* (Colorado Springs: NavPress, 1988), 101.

CHAPTER 7

1. Aubrey Malphurs, *Pouring New Wine Into Old Wineskins: How to Change a Church without Destroying It* (Grand Rapids, Mich.: Baker Books, 1993), 100–106.

CHAPTER 9

1. Christian A. Schwarz, *Natural Church Development: A Guide to Eight Essential Qualities of Healthy Churches* (Carol Stream, Ill.: Churchsmart Resources, 1996).
2. Ibid., 53.
3. John C. Maxwell, *The 21 Irrefutable Laws of Leadership: Follow Them and People Will Follow You*, rev. ed. (Nashville: Thomas Nelson, 2007), 1.
4. Wayne Schmidt and Yvonne Prowant, *Accountability: Becoming People of Integrity* (Indianapolis, Ind.: Wesley Press, 1991).
5. Bill Hybels and Mark Mittelberg, *Becoming a Contagious Christian* (Grand Rapids, Mich.: Zondervan, 1994).
6. Jim Collins, *Good to Great: Why Some Companies Make the Leap . . . and Others Don't* (New York: HarperCollins, 2001), 41.

CHAPTER 10

1. Daniel Goleman, *Working with Emotional Intelligence* (New York: Bantam Books, 1998).

CHAPTER 11

1. Richard A. Swenson, *Margin: How to Create the Emotional, Physical, Financial, and Time Reserves You Need* (Colorado Springs: NavPress, 1992).
2. Henry Blackaby, Richard Blackaby, and Claude King, *Experiencing God: Knowing and Doing the Will of God*, rev. ed. (Nashville: B&H, 2008).

CHAPTER 12

1. F. John Reh, "Pareto's Principle—The 80/20 Rule," accessed August 23, 2010, http://management.about.com/cs/generalmanagement/a/Pareto081202.htm.

CHAPTER 13

1. Jim Collins, *Good to Great: Why Some Companies Make the Leap . . . and Others Don't* (New York: HarperCollins, 2001), 126.
2. "The Emerging Role of the Executive Pastor," Defining Moments audio series (South Barrington, Ill.: Willow Creek Association, 2002).

CHAPTER 14

1. Bruce Rosenstein, "Scandals Nothing New to Business Guru," *USA Today*, July 5, 2002, http://www.usatoday.com/money/general/2002.07/05/2002-07-05-drucker.htm.
2. Richard Zalack, *Are You Doing Business or Building One?: How to Turn Your Business Into Your Benefactor* (Brunswick, Ohio: Praxis Press, 2000), 30.
3. Ibid., 15.

CHAPTER 15

1. Larry L. McSwain, *Conflict Ministry in the Church* (Nashville: Broadman & Holman, 1981), 36.